# HEY BY GEORGE! IV

## *The legend continues*

GEORGE W. DENN

www.xulonpress.com

Since before time began no one has ever imagined,
No ear heard, no eye seen, a God like you who works
for those who wait for him.

~Isaiah 64:4

# TABLE OF CONTENTS

# FORWARD

To preserve the original intent of the author all stories are unedited! On Thanksgiving Day 2013 I was at some friends of mine over in Wisconsin. I was killing some time that morning by watching some movies. One of the movies I was watching was called Batman begins, as I was watching the movie I heard this quote.

"If you make yourself more than just a man, if you devote yourself to an Ideal, and if they can't stop you, then you become something else entirely, which is Legend!"

Like a light that shot through my brain at that moment God told me what the subtitle of my book should be called "The Legend Continues!" Many times I have been called a legend to my amusement, but I want to take the emphasis off myself, and put it where it rightfully belongs on Jesus Christ the true Legend of all time, who has been at work in my life since, well right from the beginning! Legend has it that my mother went with my Father to get a load of hay the day before I was born at the farm that they had previously lived on. Mother told Dad that this kid is ether going to be born or he isn't. Evidently the jostling of loading the hay and the truck ride over and back indeed started a process that made my mom inform my dad that he better hurry up and get his chores done, because this baby was finally on its way! And so it was that at 2 minutes after midnight on April 20 1962 Good Friday to be exact I came into this world. An Aunt of mine made the statement that I would become a Priest as my people were all Catholic! I did become part of the priesthood of all believers, but I doubt that was what my Aunt had in mind! After many years of working in the hay fields and after giving my life to Jesus, one thing that seemed interesting to me was that I could always see Jesus at work in my life while I was messing around with hay! This caused me to wonder for years, what is up with that? One day at church there was some musicians there, they were called the 10 mile drive. They were singing this song they had written of how when Jesus was born he was laid in the hay! At that moment something like a piercing shot of light came into my brain, and I was made to understand that Jesus is in the hay! I am amused that I was at Ray and Denise Olson's that day because they wanted me to bring them some hay for their goats, but I was really on route to go to other friends further on Tracy and Cheri Porters, but they wouldn't be able to have me come until the next day. So after all these years I can still see Jesus at work in my life while I am messing around with hay! I asked a hand full of people to help me write a forward to this book most of them I have written about somewhere in its pages, most of them I have met far from the hay fields back home. I am very honored to have come to know each of them and consider each a special friend! Let's read what each of them has to say as they too follow this same legend as I. The only reason we know each other at all is because of Jesus the Christ, the legend that has continued through the ages!

~ George W. Denn

My husband and I can't even remember the year when we first met George, it seems like we've always known him. He comes up to our place at least once a year and when he walks through the door it feels like our little brother has come to visit. He makes himself at home for a few days and we enjoy his company, playing a mean game of dominoes or listening to one of his hilarious stories. In between naps, he might even do a little fishing. One thing that always struck me about George is his ability to see God's hand in everything and I think you'll find that ringing true as you read his books. I hope you enjoy reading George's writings as much as I have and are richly blessed for it.

~Bonnie Lindquist

When I read the forward by George, I was surprised and amused to see that he quoted from the movie Batman Begins. I didn't even know George liked Batman! This book is sure to be a wonderful journey of surprise, amusement and awe in the unique relationship that Jesus and George share. As you read these stories, it's as if George were actually sitting there himself telling them to you (while you drive his pickup truck and collect the earnings from his pumpkin stands). Thanks for being truly who God made you to be George- it's a joy to be your friend.

~ Britta Lahr

When I first met George, I immediately understood he was a different kind of person.

He taught me to use his machines; he was really patient with me, because I did not know how to use them. He works harder and harder. When we picked up pumpkins, we worked all the day long.

Sometimes he woke up really early. The best thing I did with George was cut the corn with a corn binder or chainsaw. It was crazy! If you asked him his philosophy of life, he would probably answer: do not buy things you do not need, with money you do not have, to impress people who do not care. I can say only one thing for sure about George. Even if I met a lot of people in my life, I have never met a person like George. He believes in God with all his strength. He is not afraid for the future, because God is with him.

~ Giuseppe Corvo

George has had such an impact on me and my family. We have all enjoyed reading his books. My family couldn't put them down when they first came into our home. We would sit around the dinner table and read parts together, then discuss what we learned from them. Reading his books is like following along with him in an adventure story, as he faithfully walks with the Lord through life's daily trials and joys. When I think of George, the first words that stand out in my mind are generosity and faith. George truly lives a life where he is dependent on God's provision and generosity has just become a natural part of the way that he lives his life in obedience to the Lord. I have never met anyone who is more eager and willing to give generously of all that he has to demonstrate love to others and to serve the Lord. He truly brings fame to the Name of Jesus by the example of his way of life.

Through the eyes of this Minnesota pumpkin farmer, I have been blessed to see the evidence of a man who truly embodies what it is to follow Jesus Christ faithfully. I will never forget the weekend that I spent planting pumpkins with George on his farm, and especially those long drives in the pickup truck, complete with colorful stories of his adventures with the Lord. There is nothing quite like hearing his stories right from George himself, but these books come quite close. If you follow George Denn for long enough, you are sure to have an adventure right around the corner!

~Danielle Lahr

My husband Jim and I met George several years ago at Heartland SEP camp and it has been a blessing ever since. He is a very generous and kind man who loves and serves King Jesus. Now the way that we have really come to know George is through his Hey by George series. We are always excited when we receive a new email knowing we will hear what God is doing in the life of George Denn. Thank you for sharing and encouraging us in the Lord as you open your daily diary for us to read your personal journey with Jesus Christ. Keep sharing what the Master is doing in and through you George and may He bless you as you write.

~Veronica Booth

When I first met George about ten or eleven years ago at Heartland SEP camp. He gave me his first book. That was to be the beginning of a lifelong relationship. George and I have so many things in common. He reminds me so much of when I was very young. I was raised on a farm in North Carolina and when George is talking about some of the things he is doing I can relate to almost everything he has experienced. I love the way he plays cards. GOD has made this relationship. I thank GOD for bringing you into my life.

~Bernie Bryant

I have known George Denn for several years. We met through church, both being members of Grace Communion International. Also, George is a farmer and I grew up on a farm as well as working on other farms for over 40 years. George and I also have worked together at our summer church youth camp for many years.

We have worked together, played together, and reminisced about our farm experiences together. Much of our "farm talk" is centered around some very interesting and funny story-telling. His stories are always entertaining.

What is unique about George is that his stories most often relate to his relationship with God in some way. Either he tells a story of an experience and relates what he has learned about God and himself from that experience, or he actively tells a story showing how God has directly intervened in his life to help him through difficult situations and trials. The miracles God has performed for George are truly amazing.

George is a man of faith and a pleasure to spend time with. Because he is a man of faith, you will see Scripture come alive in the way he relates his experiences on the pages of this book. His books are full of the stories and experiences described above. As you read through these priceless tales, you will laugh and cry and feel many other emotions as well. Best of all, your faith in and with Jesus Christ will be strengthened through the time you spend with George, as he relives his experiences in the pages of this book. I know my life has been enriched in this way as I have spent time with George and I believe yours will be as well.

~Dave Holmes

# Hey By George! May 8-15 2012

## NEW BEGINNINGS

Genesis 12:1-4

1 God told Abram: "Leave your country, your family, and your father's home for a land that I will show you. 2 I'll make you a great nation and bless you. I'll make you famous; you'll be a blessing. 3 I'll bless those who bless you; those who curse you I'll curse. All the families of the Earth will be blessed through you." 4 So Abram left just as God said, and Lot left with him. Abram was seventy-five years old when he left Haran.

One day not long ago I started plowing on a field, on the new farm that I rented, from my friend Wayne Schwartz. Wayne was telling me that this was the first year that the farm had been run by someone other than a Schwartz in more than 100 years! This field I was plowing had been pasture for the last 20 years. But since Wayne has sold his cows and rented his farm to me, it will God willing be growing pumpkins this year! As I guided my tractor and plow back and forth across the field, it was fun to watch the green grass get turned under and watch the soft brown/black virgin soil be turned to the sun for the first time in years! Once in a while I would watch as a night crawler, who was only seconds earlier minding his own business under the soil, be eaten by a bird! Sorry Mr. Night crawler, but I have also come to know that life isn't always fair! As I was watching the soil turn it reminded me of a sharp knife cutting through a piece of angel food cake! I started getting thoughts that this would make a great story, but I thought I was done with all of that, I guess not! About the last thing I want to do is ignore the prompting's of the Holy Spirit! While thinking of all of this I thought the title New Beginnings would be appropriate. I already had 33 acres seeded to barley there on the last week of March. For some reason the season felt about a month a head of normal this year. So on the 4 of April I planted a field of corn on the other side of Lesueur County. My neighbor David Gibson tried to talk me out of it. He asked me if I was sure that I wanted to do this. I told David that normally I would agree with him that the 4th of April is way too early in southern Minnesota to be planting corn! But I was convinced that we were a month early, and the Holy Spirit was nudging me pretty good to get it planted! David told me that he would wait until the federal crop insurance date of April 11 was here before he would plant his corn. As I write this my corn is in the 3 leaf stage and David is only half done planting his corn being stopped because of too much rain! I am glad I listened to God and try not to rub it in too much to David! My friend Wayne is experiencing anxieties this spring, so I have been going over there most every day to help Wayne get the farm ready for me to farm it. Our first project was to cut up some trees and burn brush piles that had accumulated over time. I took my friend Jeff with for this project. We cut up a winter's supply of fire wood for Jeff and Wayne seems to be able to operate when friends are there, and not feel so over whelmed by everything that needs doing, so it looks like everyone wins! One day I was hauling manure something I haven't done in more than 10 years now. As I was doing this Wayne stopped to chat. He said that he was glad I liked doing this because he sure didn't! I told Wayne that I figured I was putting it on 15 tons to the acre, and that all should add up to a lot of great pumpkins, and the pumpkins go to serve the Lord. So that's what I am doing is serving the Lord! So that's why I like it! I am also meeting new people over there. A couple times I have talked to Wayne's brother Allen. He is the guy that will harvest my barley crop there. Another day I got to meet Wayne's Cousin Chuck Schwartz. Chuck is a real friendly guy and has commented that he has read some of my stories and can relate to them. Chuck was telling me some of his story's with his experiences with dairy cows! He just sold them and wonders what he will do in the future! Oh how familiar they all sound! Everyone including myself seems to be in some sort of transition these days. From the content of his story's I feel God is very active in Chuck's life and is perusing him whether or not he realizes it. One of the statements Chuck made was every time he came onto this place he always felt a warmth there!( Wayne and Chuck both call the place Uncle Adolf's something I find interesting as a guy by the name of Adolf lived on the place where I live, before we did! ) I didn't tell Chuck this but I feel he was feeling the warmth of Gods presents there. I feel very at peace when I am over there something I once felt here! Another day I was plowing some green manure down and Chuck was planting corn in afield next to where I was. Chuck stopped to talk, I was telling Chuck that sort of thing didn't happen to often any more a lot of times you don't even know the guy who farms the ground beside yours let alone stop to visit. Everyone around here seems to be very interested that I am going to be raising pumpkins over here, as well as the story's I write! It reminds me of

Luke 4:24.

24 Well, let me tell you something: No prophet is ever welcomed in his hometown.

It always seemed that there were more people back home against what I was doing than was for me? Just yesterday I was over to Wayne's place we were doing some tiling. Some of the old drainage tiles had collapsed and we had to put in some new tile so the water would drain off the field. I met a Father and son team. Brian and Randy Guertin they are from a little burg called St. Tomas about 16 miles away. They were digging the old tile up with their backhoe. Randy is 27 and worked for Wayne a few years back. Brian and Wayne went to school together. Randy was showing Wayne and me how to witch for the water lines with 2 pieces of wire. I had seen this done years ago the guy was using a willow stick, but I had no success myself. Randy was telling Wayne that he had to get in touch with his inner self, and become one with the metal wires that he held loosely in each hand. This all amused me! Wayne was walking across the field arms stretched forward both wires pointed straight ahead. As he crossed where the water line was the wires moved in his hands. The one on the left pointed to the right and the one on the right pointed to the left crossing one another! Next it was my turn, but I never had to get in touch with my inner self as I already am in touch with Jesus who lives inside of me! I walked across where the tile line should be and sure enough the wires crossed just as they had for Randy and Wayne! I was telling Randy and Brian that I had my own theory why that had worked and they would probably laugh when I told them. "What's your theory?" they asked. I said that water was the symbol of the Holy Spirit, and if Jesus was living inside of us this would be the energy that moved the wires. They didn't say a thing, but I bet they won't forget that theory! Before we quit last night we had water flowing once again from the new tile line we put in across that field. Success! Now I can continue with my plowing, as I want to start planting pumpkins next week!

1-Corinthians 9:10

10 Don't you think his concern extends to us? Of course. Farmers plow and thresh expecting something when the crop comes in.

A few weeks ago in the midst of pre pairing Wayne's farm for pumpkins, my friend Rick asked me several times if I was going to attend our regional church conference? It was to be held at the Renaissance hotel in North Brook IL. I told Rick that I hadn't even considered it! I hadn't gone to one of those things in 6 years! Rick tried several times to persuade me, but he had no success for one thing money was an issue I don't just have $500 laying around this time of year for such things so on a scale of 1-10 my chances to go to this event were a negative 3! One day I was at my computer. I happen to be reading about Denise Olson she had just went through brain surgery. They had removed an aneurysm not more than two weeks previous. The hospital set up a site where Denise could communicate with people and share her progress, and they could respond back. That day Denise was requesting prayer for relief of pain and to be able to sleep. I said a prayer for Denise and wrote to her in the journal that I had just prayed for her, and I would call her someday in the near future. For some reason I had been thinking about Denise that day I hadn't talked to her since last thanksgiving time. I had learned of her condition at camp training at the end Of March. We had just finished with a 7 person anointing session. Cherie Porter asked if anyone had heard of Denise's condition about 20 of us prayed for her healing at that time. Before I could shut off my computer my phone was ringing, it was Denise she told me that she had been thinking of calling me all day! I told Denise that I had just sent her something on her site; she said she had been off her computer for 17 minutes! We talked about many things she asked if I was going to the conference the next weekend. I said I hadn't planned on it as I only had $1 in my billfold and until God provided more I didn't figure I could get far on that! Denise asked if they could come up with the money if I would consider going then. I figured if they were going to pay me to go to the conference that probably God wanted me to go! Ray's Olson's men's group funded my meals and registration and also had a room , but I ended up staying in Gordy's room, as the one I planned on got more crowded, and Rick sent $200 for gas. I only had to drive down to Denise and Ray's and they would drive the rest of the way. We had 5 people in our group traveling to Chicago so talk was plentiful! I sure was glad that I went, I felt renewed I even for the first time in 17 years got to meet our Pastor General Joseph Tkach. He was telling me that He never laughed so hard in his life, and that his sides just ached! I think most people were just as surprised to see me there as I was to be there! Once I was there, I knew it was a God thing that I was there. Since Ray had money for me to get back home on I felt that any money I had left should be spent while at the conference. Not long after I decided that, Mary handed me a check for $100 toward help with my books! Mike handed me $50 and told me Jesus wanted me to have this, and Bernie also told me that he was having a good year, and handed me $50. I hadn't said a word to anyone about needing money, because there was no need! Jesus never ceases to amaze me! So once again I returned home with more than I went with In more ways than one! I stopped off to the Albert Lee seed house on my way home. I needed to buy 2 pounds of untreated pumpkin seed purchased with some of the money I came home with. I planted these seeds just yesterday one week after I bought them; on ground that has never had pumpkins planted on it before! As I bring this story to a close I am reminded of a statement I heard once. "If you want to see what you have never seen. Then you must do things you have never done!" Springtime what a glorious time of year a time of new beginnings!

Gods' peace to you all!

In Christ,

George Denn

Added the evening of May 15

After getting half the pumpkins planted over at Wayne's farm. David Maki and I were moving over to plant pumpkins at Joe Kruse's farm. We were about half way home when right in front of us a Tahoe speed across the road right in our path. David said "this doesn't look good! Stop George! Stop!" We saw the wheels turn quickly and the car bolted back across the road just missing us by a few feet spin around land in the ditch and flipped over once sideways and land in some ones yard on its wheels facing the opposite direction! David Ran to see if the driver was ok and I called the cops. The driver was severely shook up, but not badly hurt! The young couple to whom the lawn belonged too came from the house to see what had happened. I introduced myself. Right away they asked me if I was the guy who wrote the book. I said yes actually I said I had three of them now. They said they always come and buy pumpkins from me. The lady was taken to the hospital in an ambulance and we had to tell the cop what we had seen. It was such a beautiful day when it started. I never would have guessed it came very close to being my last! I guess it just wasn't my time yet!

Psalm 40:16-17

16 But all who are hunting for you–oh, let them sing and be happy. Let those who know what you're all about tell the world you're great and not quitting. 17 And me? I'm a mess. I'm nothing and have nothing: make something of me. You can do it; you've got what it takes–but God, don't put it off.

# Hey by George! July 9- August 19 2012

## Answered Prayers, Mysteries Reveled and a Whole Lot of Fun Part-1

Psalm 65

A David Psalm

1-2 Silence is praise to you, Zion-dwelling God,

And also obedience.

You hear the prayer in it all.


2-8 We all arrive at your doorstep sooner

or later, loaded with guilt,

Our sins too much for us—

but you get rid of them once and for all.

Blessed are the chosen! Blessed the guest

at home in your place!

We expect our fill of good things

in your house, your heavenly manse.

All your salvation wonders
are on display in your trophy room.
Earth-Tamer, Ocean-Pourer,
Mountain-Maker, Hill-Dresser,
Muzzler of sea storm and wave crash,
of mobs in noisy riot —
Far and wide they'll come to a stop,
they'll stare in awe, in wonder.
Dawn and dusk take turns
calling, "Come and worship."


9-13 Oh, visit the earth,
ask her to join the dance!
Deck her out in spring showers,
fill the God-River with living water.
Paint the wheat fields golden.
Creation was made for this!
Drench the plowed fields,
soak the dirt clods
With rainfall as harrow and rake
bring her to blossom and fruit.
Snow-crown the peaks with splendor,
scatter rose petals down your paths,
All through the wild meadows, rose petals.
Set the hills to dancing,
Dress the canyon walls with live sheep,
a drape of flax across the valleys.
Let them shout, and shout, and shout!
Oh, oh, let them sing!

One of the busiest times of the year for me is early summer when haying time begins. This year especially as it is the first year in 17 years that I don't have a full time hired man working for me! Another thing I notice is that whenever I cut hay it almost always wants to rain, before I can get it put up! I am starting to think it just does this to aggravate me! This year the day before I cut 78 acres of red clover I got 1.25 inches of rain. It didn't rain there for another 2 weeks, so with God's help I got 1st crop hay put up in perfect shape, which is normally a pretty easy sell. I had in mind calling a few people to see if they may want to buy it, but right now I am on this kick of listening to God before I head out on my own direction. The prayer probably went something like this as I have forgotten my exact words. Father God, Jesus, and Holy Spirit I have many people in mind to call about this hay I thank you for letting me get it put up with no rain and if it's your will I ask that you send me the person that you want to buy this hay in Jesus name amen. I was thinking it sure would be nice to not have to put all this in the shed. After that I went about my day. I had it in mind if I could sell this crop for $150 a ton I would, if not I will put it in the shed, but selling it now would help me much financially! That afternoon I got a call from Travis Shirping from Albany MN, Travis's Dad bought some hay about 5 years ago but I only thought of those guys in passing thought as they had this neighbor whom they had been buying from since. After several calls back and forth Travis decided he would buy the hay from me! Thank you Jesus!!!!! This would set me up financially until grain harvest time. On one of the weekends in June while I was cutting some of the 50 acres of wild hay that I put up. The Mankato airport was putting on an air show it was interesting driving around the area seeing thousands of people parked everywhere looking to the sky even people I did not know came into my yard they were parked in my drive way. I just laughed as two girls in bikinis waved at me as I drove out my driveway. I had a wedding to go to, and I have seen air shows before. The site of it all reminded me of the return of Jesus. An air show no one will miss!

Luke 21:25-28

25 "It will seem like all hell has broken loose–sun, moon, stars, earth, sea, 26 in an uproar and everyone all over the world in a panic, the wind knocked out of them by the threat of doom, the powers-that-be quaking. 27 "And then–then!–they'll see the Son of Man welcomed in grand style–a glorious welcome! 28 When all this starts to happen, up on your feet. Stand tall with your heads high. Help is on the way!"

Another day Chris Schenk and his dad Allen were baling hay for me across the road in Fred's slough. The hay was ready but we had no sunshine, only clouds and a little bit of a breeze. So the hay was a little bit tough. To help dry the hay I hitched my pickup to the hay rake and raked all the hay once again before the baler when I got done I parked at the edge of the field. I fell asleep for a short time, and when I woke up I could see they needed another hayrack. I went up to the yard to get one and when I got back Chris and Allen said I just missed all the excitement! Apparently after I had left the field somebody had drove off the road and jumped the drainage ditch and landed right where I and my pickup had been siting only minutes before. I asked what happened to the person. Evidently they just drove out of the hay field and drove away! That's the second time in a month I was almost hit by a vehicle! I sort of get the feeling someone is trying to take me out! All afternoon we seemed like we were on the edge of a system. I could see it was probably raining hard over at Wayne's farm where the pumpkins are. I was telling Chris that it seemed God was holding back the weather for us. Chris didn't believe that he figure that was just the way it is. But I know Allen knew it too I could see it in his face. We finished with the field and it immediately started to rain we could bale no more hay that day! The rest would have to wait a few days, when we could my neighbor David Just got the rest baled and there was water siting in the field the next day! The Morning after Chris and Allen baled Fred's slough. Wayne Schwartz called I asked him how he was doing as he didn't sound too good. Not good Wayne said we got an awful lot of hail here last night the barley was flattened and the pumpkins are all smashed! I immediately called David Holmes and Doug Johannsen to send this out on a prayer request as I carry no farm insurance on the crops! This is a whole other story how he brought me to this, but God is my insurance I only carry that which is required. I wasn't too worried about the pumpkins as they are pretty tough. I had an insurance adjuster tell me one time that pumpkins needed to be 80% hailed out before they even started to pay out on them because of their ability to re-vine! The barley however is not tough at all I didn't even go over there for 3 days to look at it as I was too busy doing stuff over here, besides it was so wet over there that I couldn't do anything anyway, and after last year the news hardly fazed me anyway I figure God knows what he is up too! I highly doubt that God would move me over to Wayne's just so he could ruin me when he already had me ruined last year! As I write this the pumpkins have come back from the hail and the barley will be harvested this week while I'm at Northern light camp. I did have this strange thing happen to me one day. About a week before camp I was cultivating pumpkins the way my rows are every other row I have to make 3 passes with the cultivator between the rows. I know that I had only made 2 passes on the previous row, so I had to go back down that row, because I had skipped over to one that needed only 2 passes, but when I looked over there the row had been cultivated, but I had not done it! Also I cultivated all 68 acres of pumpkins and squash this year in just 3 days normally it takes 5 so I would say. It must be God helping me, or I am going nuts! There is no other explanation. This year at Northern light camp I was to do a class on writing. The folks who put the camp together wanted some sort of plan from me how I would take the class I had none and nothing was coming until I took Dad up to Gordy's fishing the weekend before camp. There God gave the direction to take the class as well as a name I should call it inspired writing as I have never wrote anything unless I was Inspired to write it. I was sort of fearful no one would sign up for my class it was advertised this way. Check out Georges inspired writing class and leave with far more treasure then you came with! I only had 2 people sign up, but others came and we ended up with 6 people. Today Doug's boys Josh, Hunter, Scott, and William made me a rope 145 feet long we were thinking of having a tug of war with it across the root river, but that never materialized! God has been answering my prayers every day for my inspirational writing class. My class consisted of Morgan, Jessica, Vivian, Muriel, John, and Richard. Ted and Linda Gamble also took part for a session. The first day was called getting started. It was interesting that very morning down in the lounge we were all there and Becky Duel asked me where Lake Crystal Minnesota was, as a Darlene Woods Commented on something she had on face book. Darlene was the person who it was because of that I wrote anything in the first place! What are the odds of that happening on the first day of my class! I gave everyone in my class a copy of my first book Hey by George! I read to them my very first story I wrote, and another one I had written after I had quit writing the first time. Then the last half of the class was devoted for them to write their stories. Something they could keep working on in class all week. The second day the topic was finding a style all your own. This day each person received the second book of mine. I read them the story of an old pickup I once had we nicknamed "the Hammer" The second story I read them was from pages 47-53 which was actually 4 separate stories. One of the 4 stories was the story of the $2 bill so I gave every one a $2 bill from 1976. The 3 day we continued on with developing your own style a gift of my third book was given and the last story from it was read. The 4 Th day I covered epilogs and forwards. Each person was given a homemade pen that I got from Doug Johannsen. Doug just happened to have 7 pens from 7 different kinds of wood in his pickup! I presented each pen with the spiritual significance that God has given us each a unique life now it is up to us to share our stories with others. The fifth day I went over publishing and a $2 gift certificate to the camp store was given to each with the spiritual significance to go out and make a difference in your world! Each person had been working on a story of their own and testimonies were given later that evening at the Symposium. I was touched to find out several of the stories would not have been written had they not attended the class! One of the people I met for the first time this year was Nathan Keating from San Diego California. Nathan is the fourth person I know from there. Two campers Alex and Connor are from there, and Paul Schwartz is stationed at camp

Pendleton. Nathan is involved with Generations ministries which is part of Grace Communion International sponsored camps. Nathan led worship for us every day he had this song that he wrote, and we all sang every day 'Rooted' was based on psalm 1

1 Blessed is the man Who walks not in the counsel of the ungodly, Nor stands in the path of sinners, Nor sits in the seat of the scornful; 2 But his delight is in the law of the Lord, And in His law he meditates day and night. 3 He shall be like a tree Planted by the rivers of water, That brings forth its fruit in its season, Whose leaf also shall not wither; And whatever he does shall prosper. 4 The ungodly are not so, But are like the chaff which the wind drives away. 5 Therefore the ungodly shall not stand in the judgment, Nor sinners in the congregation of the righteous. 6 For the Lord knows the way of the righteous, But the way of the ungodly shall perish

It is one of those songs that sticks in your head and you can't get it out! Here it is.

Rooted(Psalm 1) by Nathan Keating
Verse 1:
I wanna be rooted, deep in Your love
Forever planted, standing firm in Your Word
I won't be shaken, no I'll never move
As long as I am rooted in you
Verse 2:
I wanna be rooted, in pastures of grace
Forever growing, until I see Your face
I'm givin' You glory, with Your mercies anew
As long as I am rooted in You
Chorus:

Like a tree by living waters

Forever sustained by You

On Your Word I am standing, in faith I am planted

My heart wants to be

I wanna be rooted

Hip-hop 1:

In Your ways, oh Lord, my soul delights

Your Word is like a lamp unto my feet

Like the moonlight so I recite

Meditatin' day and night, soarin' to new heights

Verse 3:

I wanna be rooted, in Your triumphant hand

With the strength of Your promise, in victory I'll stand

Whatever the battle, no, I'll never lose

As long as I am rooted in You

Hip-hop 2:

Suited and booted, I'm rooted in the Lion of Judah

With livin' waters flowin' through these veins

It's like I'm soarin' in an airplane high up in the sky

I'm deeply rooted in His Word, in Him I will abide

One-third the trinity put within me

So I'll stand as firm as can be

let the wicked take heed

Only one way to find true life is only found in David's seed

Outro

I wanna be rooted

Rooted, deep in Your love

I wanna be rooted

Firm in Your Word

I wanna be rooted

In victory I'll stand

I wanna be rooted

Rooted in You


By the end of camp I had given Nathan my 3 books and I got a couple of his CDs. I found out later that Nathan would also be at Heartland camp which was in 2 weeks. Ross Jutsum was also there for part of the week. I had met Ross about 12 years ago. At that time Ross had told the story of how he had fallen off a ladder and broke both of his wrists. As a piano player this had been a huge Trial/test for Ross! And like us all Ross was wondering what God was up to in his life at that time. His Chinese doctor at that time reminded Ross of how God watches over the little birds.

> Matthew 6:25-27
> 25 "Therefore I say to you, do not worry about your life, what you will eat or what you will drink; nor about your body, what you will put on. Is not life more than food and the body more than clothing? 26 Look at the birds of the air, for they neither sow nor reap nor gather into barns; yet your heavenly Father feeds them. Are you not of more value than they? 27 Which of you by worrying can add one cubit to his stature?

She told him that he was big bird and that God would see him through this trial. I was telling Ross one morning at coffee time that he had no idea how many times that I had told people that story over the years! I believe we all must go through times of suffering it's important that we do however sometimes we try to avoid it because none of us wants to suffer and by doing so we settle for a life of mediocrity! One day at chapel I had just been talking with someone about Jack Hayford and how much over the years I have gotten something out of his ministry. Ross had heard me talking about Jack and he turned around and told me that Jack Hayford was a personal friend of his; needless to say that pretty much impressed me! It is always hard to leave camp. As I was heading home Doug Johannsen called me to see if I was up to lunch. I was so we stopped at a Culver's in Rochester. We had hardly sat down when Josh Craig walked up, and said hi to us. Josh was a former camper from several years back, and was now working at Culver's. It was good to see Josh again I always wondered what he was up to!

Part 2 Answered prayers, Mysteries Reveled and a whole lot of fun!

I left Doug and William and headed for home! I waited until I was out of Rochester to turn my cell phone back on, back to the real world I said to myself. Almost immediately it started ringing it was Albert Block the guy who was to harvest my wheat. He informed me that he was heading to the first field to start combining wheat in less than an hour, so I had to make some phone calls! I had to call Howard Guse to get his tractor and grain cart over to my place, and to Chris Schenk to bring semi's to dump the wheat into. These arrangements were all made before camp so everyone was ready to respond when I called them depending on when Albert was ready to start. I find these days the most important machine I run is my cell phone. I guess my younger brother was right after all, he made the statement once that all I liked to do was drink coffee and talk on the telephone! There is more truth in that statement today than when it was made! I had just 10 days to get $50,000 worth of crops harvested before heartland camp. Can I get all of that done? Not without Gods help! My neighbor David was just about finished cutting my second crop hay that I hired him to do, when I pulled up to the field I haven't even made it home yet, and can see God working things out for me. Albert got the wheat harvested in 2 days it went 33 bushel an acre, and sold for $10.08 per bushel. Not the best yield, but it was the best price I had ever got for wheat. By the next weekend we had the straw and the hay all baled! About the time we started to bale the hay I said, "Lord it sure would be nice if a buyer for this crop of hay would come along. So I don't have to go through all the work of putting this in the shed." That afternoon Travis Schirping called me again to see if I had any more hay that I wanted to sell. After 3 days Travis decided he would buy the hay! I know this is from God as here is the arrangement that was made. I asked Travis what the first crop had cost him with the trucking "$174 dollars a ton" Travis said. I had received $150 a ton for the hay. I told Travis that my lowest price this time would be $175 a ton, but I would pay for half the trucking this time. Travis actually paid less for this hay and I received more $162.50 per ton. $22,000 for this crop paid in cash money which has put me in the best financial shape in my entire life! Another thing I found interesting was we got exactly the same amount of bales as the 1st crop, but they weighed 200 pounds more each. Which is very odd, I have put up a lot of hay in my lifetime and I don't think I have ever seen such a thing. The first crop had all the spring rains, but the second crop only had 7 tenths of an inch of rain! So I definitely see Gods hand a work with the hay as it was nothing

I did! The barley on Wayne's farm that got the hail was harvested while I was at northern light camp they put all 600 bushel in a bin, and the straw was baled and sold a lite crop at best. The pumpkins though appear to be one of the best crops ever; hopefully this is not just a mirage! Thursday morning the morning before I was to leave for Heartland camp I loaded the last load of round bales onto Jason Shirping's semi-truck. Jason is a cousin to Travis both live near St. Cloud Minnesota. Before we started to load Jason handed me an envelope it was the second half of the payment for the hay. I handed it to Dad and told him to count it while I loaded the hay. My Dad is 81 years old and I know that was the most cash he had ever held at one time in his life! I want to mention something here that may be significant to someone who reads this. When I was 30 years old I bought Dad's share of the farming operation. At that time my Dad financed $50,000 of it interest free. Right after that I was fined by the DNR for allegedly polluting the lake out here, which eventually lead to bankruptcy 10 years later. The $50,000 was never taken care of by me. After a while I was just going to let it slide, because I had seen my Dad do that very thing to his Dad with $5,000. Once in a while this was bought up, but my Father always said that wasn't as much as I owed him. That is true, but I know to Grandpa Denn $5000 was a lot of money! One day around 2 years ago God showed me that I needed to change my thinking on this and make an attempt to pay dad back. Ever since that time things seem to be going better for me.

Exodus 20:12

12 "Honor your father and your mother, that your days may be long upon the land which the Lord your God is giving you.

I just wanted to share with you my bible's foot note on this verse. "The term honor means to treat with significance. It is the opposite of in vain. Care of one's elderly parents was a basic element of social responsibility and godly piety in Israel. Here it is tied to how a person would fare in the land! People who were faithless to God by disregarding their parents would not last long in the new Promised Land. I find that interesting and encourage anyone reading this to at least make an attempt to rectify that which is between you and your parents. It may be the very thing that is keeping you from being blessed!

Part 3 Answered prayers, Mysteries reveled, and a whole lot of fun!

Dad and I left for Heartland camp in Illinois around 7 am Friday July 27. I know a lot of people who look forward to this week all year long. Every year I wonder if I should keep doing camp it is very hectic doing 2 camps right around summer harvest time! But every year I commit myself, and every year I see God re arrange my work load. Never once in all these years has anything been lost because I went to camp. When they are done they have been a rewarding experience and I am always glad I came! It probably is the most important thing I do all year long! I will say though this is the first year everything got done that needed to before I left, and there was nothing that needed doing until I got home, so that was a first! This year I had to take a load of fall decorations with to decorate the dining hall for the western theme at the dance that was to be on Wednesday evening. I was loaded down with hay bales/corn and wheat bundles, and pumpkins! I left my Dad with my cousins in Dwight Illinois and proceeded to the camp. It sure was great to see everyone again! On Saturday Tracy porter was grilling steaks and sweet corn for everyone. I was sure looking forward to that, but shortly before we ate, I got a severe head ache. Susie gave me some aspirin, but I also asked Israel to anoint me. I had 2 bites of the steak and 2 bites of sweet corn, but I was too sick to eat! I gave Nathan my steak and I went down to my dorm and slept until 6:30 the next morning. I woke up feeling great, but I put more stock in the anointing that I had then the pills that I took! I was sitting at chapel the next morning and Britta sat down beside me I was interested in hearing how her urban summit adventure went. She kind of laughed and said it was an adventure! She told a few of her experiences, but didn't have too much to say about it at that time. I was telling Britta that my first experience with inner city youth was at Snow Blast with a kid named RJ. RJ was about 14 years old when I met him and twice as big as me. His first words to me were, I could beat you up if I wanted too! Looking to the Holy Spirit for the words my immediate response was "you do and you'll wish you hadn't!" That statement disarmed RJ I never had a bit of trouble with him all the years he was at the camps, and he always gives me a hug when I see him! I think RJ has a couple of kids now so who knows maybe they will come through camp at some point. That story reminds me of another one. 9 years ago we had tent camping as one of the outdoor activities I think I was supposed to be the person in charge of that at that time? As I recall 1b was out there that night and there councilors were trying everything to get these young guys to settle down for the evening. It was past mid night and they even had their councilors in tears a couple times. These were just young guys 18 or 19 years old, but they couldn't get anyone to settle down, and I had enough! God give me wisdom how to handle this situation? Then I sprang into action I went over to the last tent this kid in there was shining his flashlight to the tent across from him and talking to the kid over there. I just knelt down at that tent and said kid if you don't shut that flashlight off and shut up and go to bed. I am going to come in there and rip your head off! Instantly the light went out and not a peep was herd from that tent the rest of the night and the whole camp just quieted right down. Thank you Jesus! They didn't have any councilor training sessions for me they just put me in those roles and with God's help I came through them all unscathed! It kind of reminds me how I learned to swim. My dad would throw us in water over our heads and would laugh about that, but we sure didn't as he hollered "swim!"

> Mathew 11:18-19
> 18 For John came neither eating nor drinking, and they say, 'He has a demon.' 19 The Son of Man came eating and drinking, and they say, 'Look, a glutton and a winebibber, a friend of tax collectors and sinners!' But wisdom is justified by her children."

I figure you can't go wrong listening to what God wants you to do in a situation. I eventually learned how to swim. RJ Grew up and had kids of his own, and Coulter Meisner just became a co-councilor and was baptized up at Northern light camp this past year. Coulter was one of those little guys from 1b that was in the tents. It sure is rewarding to see Guys that were once in my dorms when I was in a councilor role. Now are councilors themselves. I can't remember Jordan Porter ever getting into any kind of trouble. Quentin Woods the only time was the time he jumped onto the top off the golf cart I was driving and the whole top busted off! I can't remember if Quentin got punished for that, but being his uncle was camp director

I bet he got a talking too! I remembered that about Quentin the day he mentioned that he had a youth that needed to hang around me for punishment. I thought about it and told Quentin that I didn't have much going on that day, but David Worsfold had a bunch of stuff that needed to be cleaned, and I could think of no greater punishment than that! As usual driving the gator around and having this giant hill to climb was too much of a temptation for me! Dave Salander was with me one morning hauling drinks to the various activities. I always believe in making your work fun I do that at home and I do that at camp. All I did was turn down the path that the hill was on and 72 year old David jumped out of the gator he said he would have no part of that hill! For an explanation of that I will refer you to page 46 of Hey By George! III. Another day I and Joseph Porter was with taking water down to paintball. I was asking Joseph if he was up to a hill climb. "Sure George I like the way you think." Joseph said. We got over to where the hill was, but we had to wait for the mini campers to make there decent down the hill. I locked the transmission and put the thing in low, and zoomed right up the hill until we got to the top and spun out we could go no farther. I thought I just hate it when this happens! I had to back down the hill which is extremely dangerous! I got about half way down when I decided to try and turn it around. Joseph almost jumped out I told him not to do that as he was the only weight on that side! Joseph doesn't weigh all that much put every pound counted at this point! When we got to the bottom of the hill we noticed that I hadn't put it in 4 wheel drive! No wonder we hadn't made it. After the 4 wheel drive was locked we had to wait for the mini campers again this time they were climbing the hill. This time assisted by 4 wheel drive and being cheered on by the mini campers we made the climb without a hitch! One person we didn't impress all that much was Joseph's mom! My mom was the same way for some reason they always think you may get killed doing stuff like that!

One of the open activities this year was paint ball. I drive one of the vehicles that take the campers and staff down there. Staff are welcome to play so I generally stick around and play the game. One day the girls were down there and one of the girls from Britta's dorm walked up and asked if I was the person who bought blizzards for the whole dorm. I asked this young lady what would make her think that I would do that. "Because," she said. "You are so mysterious." I pretty much had all I could do to keep from cracking up with laughter at this point! My life is an open book literally! If people feel I am mysterious or unapproachable then they really don't know me at all! I suppose that after having 2 broken hearts in one life time, and not being sure if my heart could stand the aggravation of it all again! I could appear guarded or mysterious to women! I was listening to one of my favorite radio pastors the other morning, Pastor Ford. He was saying that he got this book called "Everything men know about women" it cost $14.99 and someone gave it to him for his birthday. When you open up the book there is nothing in its pages! So I guess that makes us even, women seem very mysterious to me, and I really don't want to be clobbered by one again! But to answer this young lady's question yes it was me, but not only for her dorm, but all the others as well! I didn't do it to impress anyone I did that because right know things are going as well for me as they have in my entire life! I wanted to give a gift to the camp for all the years it has given to me. So I thought what better way than to give it than through the store. I can touch each camper's life if only in a small way while I'm at camp and donate to the camp at the same time. Jesus was like that he gave us all the gift of grace even if we didn't deserve it which most of us didn't! And Jesus seemed to spend a lot of his time around the market place! And isn't that the goal to become more like Jesus? Another day at paint ball I was talking to Mrs. Barnhill, and sharing some of the stories about the pumpkins I raise, and how I market them. She in turn told those stories to her husband Jim the care taker of the Salvation Army camp. There is some land not being used at camp so they are pretty sure they are going to try their hand at raising pumpkins next year! Jim and I looked over some of the ground that they would use and I would say it should grow pumpkins just fine!

Adam Lattimore was one off the crew members this past year. "Crew is the name of the program that is used to transition those that were campers into staff positions. James Newby was kidding Adam one evening and called him "Big Al" after his initials. Adam is one big guy and the nick name stuck! Big Al liked the security run late at night so much that he rode with several of us over the course of the week on the gator and helped deliver water to several of the activities. I told Big Al one night on a security run that if he saw people up and about after they should be in bed all he needed to remember to holler the words "Go to bed!"

One night Steve and big Al was doing the security run it was about midnight and I was pretending to be some kind of spook, out in the lawn near my dorm! "Go to bed!" I heard Big Al cry out as they tried to narrowly miss me as they drove by! I do believe I have that young man trained! On Friday we had our final banquet, the theme this year was Hawaiian! Once again I was a server, but not having a Hawaiian shirt I got one from Lyne Paul. It must have been on the racy side for some, because Pastor Karl asked me if I thought it was appropriate to ware. I looked at the shirt and summarized that if one walked by the pool on any given day this past week you would have seen much similar sites! Needless to say when I got into this attire it was much different than the bib overalls people are used to seeing me in! I think I told a few people that I can't dress like this all the time as it would be too much for everyone! For the sake of not appearing mysterious I am going to disclose why I ware bib overalls.

Reason no. 1. It helps me to stay connected to my past most of the men that I knew at the time wore them including myself. It was a time when real men had real work to do, and if I would ware what most do today I would get real hurt, real fast!

Reason no. 2. It helps me to distinguish between my good clothes and work cloths seldom if ever would you see me ware them at public gatherings of any importance.

Reason no. 3. I just got tired of my pants falling down all the time, and they are very comfortable.

I did have an instance during serving that was amusing to me, but embarrassing to a camper. I was pouring water into this young gentleman's glass when I suddenly noticed the water running down the side of the pitcher pouring onto the kid's lap that sat beside him! He was embarrassed and rightly so, but I think he was the kid that Quentin was having some trouble with so I may have just cooled him down a little!

It is always a bitter sweet day the last day of camp. We start with hauling luggage up to the parking lot and you just know the end is inevitable, but you also get to see what God has accomplished throughout the week in the campers in the staff, and in yourself! It generally is a lot to take in! You also get to know the people that have been your friends for years better and those friendships deepen, and you always meet new people every year to add to your cache of friends. The end does come though, and one by one you see them leave after I dropped big Al off at the parking lot I told Tracy Porter that I had to get out of here before I bawled my head off! This year after our final meeting and about as many good- bye's as a heart can take Jordan Porter road with me and I followed Tracy and Cheri Porter out. We were all going to Stephen and Lilly Hill's place. Lilly had invited me for many years, but this was the first year I didn't have to hurry home for anything! We all spent the evening and after break-fast the next morning it was time to say good bye to these brothers and sisters, and go to my Cousin Nancy's place some 16 miles east to get my Dad. Like I said there was nothing to hurry home for so Nancy took us to the beach the next day on Lake Michigan some place in Indiana. Another first for me I mean going to the beach on Lake Michigan, I've been to Indiana before. Where we were at you could look off to your left and see Chicago across the water, and look out to your right across the water and see Michigan City. The next day we drove the 8 hours home through the parched cornfields of Illinois, Wisconsin and Minnesota every once in a while that song of Nathan's would pop into my head

"Like a tree by Living waters forever sustained by you on your word I am standing in faith I am planted my heart wants to be. I want to be rooted."

I guess hearing it so much in the past month it kind of got stuck in my head! When I got home I noticed some vines dying out in my pumpkins and by Saturday I could tell that this virus had gotten worse I decided not to take any chances and sent out to friends everywhere to pray about this virus, because I don't much like the thought of 70% of my income for the year disappearing if it can be prayed for and stopped. I and many others prayed about this virus on Monday I had organic inspection over there and they looked no better or worse. On Thursday evening I took a hay rake over to that farm as I had some hay over there just about ready to put up, and you could hardly see any dead vines! Miraculous I would say God saved the pumpkins! And many thanks to all who prayed!

I got this cool card several months back, it was probably one of the best ones any one has ever sent me! It was from a young person that I have come to know, someone that I would call a friend! In the card this scripture was wrote.

"Since ancient times no one has heard, no ear has perceived, no eye has seen any God besides you, who acts on behalf of those who wait for him. " Isaiah 64:4

This I would have to say is true! But as for this young friend of mine, seems kind of mysterious to me!

God's blessings and peace to you all!

In Christ ~George Denn

# TO EVERYTHING THERE IS A SEASON!

Luke 13:18-19

18 Then He said, "What is the kingdom of God like? And to what shall I compare it? 19 It is like a mustard seed, which a man took and put in his garden; and it grew and became a large tree, and the birds of the air nested in its branches."

Although pumpkins don't have the smallest of seeds they seem to vine out and produce fruit in the most unusual places! This year they have as far as I know have affected people from as far away as Sweden as well as Africa! To see this ministry grow from 9 corn bundles and sales of $49 and just me 17 years ago, to $113,000 in gross sales 68 acres of pumpkins, and as many as 16 people working for me in a single day, this year truly makes me give glory to God, because it is beyond anything that I could have mustered or even dreamed of within myself! And to see Father God, Jesus, and Holy Spirit at work in the people that work for me, as well as those who buy the fall stuff even in the pickups that haul the pumpkins on a daily bases is nothing short of miraculous! I will try my best to represent this as I write this story. I have to warn you though that like a pumpkin vine it probably will vine out in various directions, and if it produces any fruit than I can truly say that God caused it to do that!

So we will start off with what I call the ministry!

It was named the ministry of Joy by Pastor Doug Johannsen several years ago when he exclaimed after a visit here that you sure cause a lot of people Joy with those pumpkins George! A couple of comments that were overheard by myself and others will attest to that "This is better than Valley Fair!" said one child. "It pays for the gas to come out here in just the price alone!" said an elderly woman. If one lingers at one of the stands very long you will see cars pull up with people of any age with expressions of pure Joy all over their faces! This is all an answer to a prayer I prayed many years ago. Many people I had seen quit farming as there was no money it; it was their sole reason for quitting and going elsewhere. I enjoyed farming; money was never a part of the reason why I did so. It was me through and through and I always felt free being a farmer with no one to answer too, but the Almighty himself. When that way of life became threatened I humbled myself to that great Creator and said "Lord if it be your will please give me something that I could do to glorify you right here by what I do in Jesus name amen!" I am reminded of something it says in the Catholic bible in the book of

Sirach chapter 7 verse 15 "Hate not laborious tasks, nor farming, which was ordained by the Most High."

I never wanted to run off to some other country to serve God, turns out He made what I was doing get to other country's anyway! So that is my ultimate goal to glorify God {in this I mean God the

Father, Jesus the son, and the Holy Spirit}. So I don't do this for the money, but it is through this ministry that God allows me to make the bulk of my yearly income! One of the ways I have learned to glorify God in what I do is to give the books I have written about his working in my life away free of charge. They are the first thing to be put on the stands when they go up and the last thing to be taken off when they are taken down! More than a year ago God impressed upon me that my books are unique stories, and I should just give them away to people instead of trying to sell them, and if I would do that, He would cause money to come in from other avenues! This year I gave over 1000 books away and God caused my business to rise by 46%! So I have no reason to believe God isn't keeping his part of the bargain!

> Proverbs 23:23
> 23 Buy truth–don't sell it for love or money buy wisdom, buy education, buy insight.

That's what I feel I do the stories are true, and I do buy them for a cost! A plaque near the books introduces them this way.
A Ministry of Joy!

> Once again fall is upon us it is my favorite time of year! It is a labor of love that I continue to do this, and Gods will. As you can read about in my third book, in its last two chapters, this all came very close to not being! God spoke to me over a year ago that I should give these books away, because they are unique stories, and if I would do that, He would provide me income from other areas! God has not let me down,

and it is because of that promise that I offer these three books free of charge! It is my hope that as you walk amongst the fall decor that you not only enjoy the experience, but that you too, will experience our triune God as I have come to know him, and have written about in these three books. To God be the glory ~ George W Denn

Like I had mentioned earlier one only has to stick around the stands for a short time to see the pure joy people of all ages experience as they browse the pumpkin patches, shopping, taking pictures, or just

Looking at all the shapes sizes and colors! All this extra stuff comes with no additional charge so a family can have a free outing if they want. I have suggested prices but the size and what they pay is up to the integrity of the buyer, as no one mans the stands, and a sign that says "Pay Here" with an arrow to the slot in the money box is all it tells people to do! I try not to have expectations, and try to be satisfied by whatever God has given me that day. For all I know it is him putting money in the boxes! All I know is every night for 61 days I drive the 72 miles something I call "The run" and there is money in every box! One night I was collecting money down by my house. My land lord Wayne Schwartz was with me. When a 75 year old lady, of Methodist persuasion introduced herself. She was telling us that she enjoyed reading my stories. She also told us that she had been attending church all her life and had yet to have experiences with the Lord like I have had! Another day my friend Jeff was visiting with a 90 year old lady from the Lutheran faith. She was telling Jeff that reading my stories caused her to want to get to know the Lord better! All I can say is I am just writing these story's down about God working in my life as they happen. I really don't go out looking for more to write about! But happen they do, one day I was in my house about mid-October around 2 in the afternoon. My cell phone started ringing it was from a man that was down at my stand near Beuford. He was asking me if I was some kind of minister or something as he was standing there reading some of my stories! No I said I was just a farmer who wrote about my experiences with God! He then asked me for a job. I told him I couldn't give him one because I had too many people working for me as it was; besides my work would be done in 2 weeks! He then proceeded to tell me that he didn't want to lose his house. I assured him that I watched as everything I had worked for got taken away from me once upon a time! I also told him that it was the best thing that happened. I can say that now, I couldn't then, as the experience of it all was rather traumatic! I told him that I could sympathize with him, but could not help him. I asked if I could pray for him, which he let me! Several times there were notes in the box that simply said "God bless you sir" or just "God bless you!" I was sharing those notes with the folks that were working for me one morning. That kind of note would only come from a person without the means to pay for what they got! They all seemed to sense that this was no normal job that they were working at! One day I was working at the stand below my house, a young couple was there with their child. The guy was trying to get me to come down on my price so he could afford what he wanted! I told him just to take what he wanted and come back when he had the difference! He asked if I was cool with that, sure I said I told him it is the honor system! Whether he did or not is between him and the Lord, because there is really no way to tell! One night while the guys were covering the squash I was collecting the money and some lady stopped she asked if I was closing up for the night. No I said we had to cover the squash as it was supposed to freeze during the night. Oh she said she just stopped by to pay for some stuff that her and her family had picked up ten days ago! They had picked up more than she had money for that day. Whatever works for you I said and thanked her for her business! About the time I had been writing this my sister Jane had called me. She was telling me about a lady that was in her shop the other day. When she paid my sister she only had a hundred dollar bill. Jane told the lady that she wouldn't be able to change that. She told Jane that was alright because she owed me 40 dollars for some stuff she got one day out at my stand and hadn't paid for it yet, and asked if Jane would see to it that I got it! I have really no idea what goes on at those stands, and to tell you the truth I don't want to know! I have enough to think of as it is! Several of my visitors told me that seeing these stands testifies to the amount of faith I have! In some ways this makes me laugh because there are days I wonder if I have any faith at all! I will say this though, I believe in Jesus Christ, and I have faith in him, and that faith has brought me this far and God willing it will take me where I need to get to!

Hebrews 12:2
2 Keep your eyes on Jesus, who both began and finished this race we're in. Study how he did it. Because he never lost sight of where he was headed–that exhilarating finish in and with God–he could put up with anything along the way: cross, shame, whatever. And now he's there, in the place of honor, right alongside God.

Since Jesus is the author and finisher of our faith any I have belongs to him any way!

Looking back at this year all I can say is it was another miraculous one! At first I didn't even have the land to grow them on which changed on the 14 day of February When I rented Wayne's farm. I almost got took out twice by automobiles. In mid-June a hail storm severely damaged the pumpkins, most of the corn and soybeans in the neighborhood had to be replanted. The barley crop I had all but was destroyed it only ran 20 bushel to the acre a fair crop would have done 50! I figured that God hadn't brought me there just so he could ruin me, because he already had me ruined a year earlier! I figured I could just sit down and say I was beat or I could call some folks to join in with me in prayer about it all. I chose the prayer because I have no farm insurance. The pumpkins recovered! After camp in August I had to ask for prayers again as I had some sort of vine disease 20% of the vines had died when I asked for prayers 10 days latter you could hardly tell any were dead at all! The end of Sept. brought bugs of biblical proportions of such I have never seen! Again I asked for prayers a week later God sent some cooler weather that kept the bugs at bay, but the weather turned real cold more prayers were said the pumpkins survived the 19 degree night and a few nights later it got down to 15 degrees! I have seen pumpkins severely damaged after a 26 degree night. So to see them come through these 2 nights of such cold is just a miracle, and did I mention it was the driest year since 1988!

The workers!

Jesus had much to say about the value of workers!

Matthew 9: 37-38

37 "What a huge harvest!" he said to his disciples.
"How few workers! 38 On your knees and pray for
harvest hands!"

That's what I did pray for some helpers and the scripture above tells me that they were all hand pick by God himself! I look upon them as the most valuable part of this ministry even more so than myself, because if it was just myself I don't think much work could have got done! They are the ones that put the meat on the bones of my Ideas! So let me introduce these important people, and I will tell you how they came to me. My friend Jeff had worked for me all season after he had stepped down from his pastor position at the Church of Christ in Eagle Lake. It was just him and me in the beginning getting the stands set up and picking the first pumpkins. One day I was at Joe Kruse's farm I had stopped in to see how the pumpkins looked over there and I stopped to visit with Joe a minute. Through the course of our conversation Joe asked if he could come back and work for me this fall. I said sure he could that encouraged me as I was wondering who else the Lord was going to send me! This would be Joe's 4th season to help me. David Maki drove down from the North Country the first week in September this would be the third year that David worked for me David is 56 years old. One day I took a wagon box back to my cousin Albert Block I had used it for some wheat seed. While we were talking he mentioned that his daughter Ashley was looking for some work this fall. So Ashley Block came and joined the group. A guy by the name of Bruce helped for 2 weeks. Bruce was living in the shed over on Doris's farm he was a good worker, but just like that he was gone! No one seems to know what happened to him not even Doris! Doris said one day he just didn't come back. One day I was talking with my neighbor David Scholtz on my home stand he asked if I could use some more help. I told David that this time of year I can use all the help I can get! About mid-September some tension arouse between Jeff and myself I could see that I was pushing everyone beyond what was possible. I had been to the bank a few weeks back, Art Colum one of the bankers there told me if I ever needed some extra help he could line up for me as many as ten workers from the Maranatha ministry's at the college here in Mankato. I called Art and told him I was interested in hiring the guys he had been talking about at the bank a few weeks back. Art mentioned that most of these would be foreign exchange students from Kenya Africa. And one day this fellow Steve called me I programmed him in my phone as Steve pumpkin pick! Steve told me he could have as many as 10 guys come on Saturdays and they would work from 8am-6:30 pm. These guys became known to us as the Kenyan's. Steve laughed when I told him that I had his name programmed as Steve pumpkin pick, because he said he had forgotten my last name also and had me programmed as George pumpkin in his phone! These 9-10 guys from various parts of Africa and the U.S. working mostly on Saturdays on just 4 weekends picked and rowed most of the pumpkins I called them pumpkin picking machines. Steve was telling me that I was quite a blessing to them. I told him that went both ways as they all were a blessing to me, because me and my crew never would have gotten it all done! Here are the names of all those we knew as the Kenyan's

Anthony Anvame–Gabon
John Tegut–Kenya

John Makabe- Kenya

Josiah–USA

Delwende–Burkina Faso

Eyasu–Ethiopia

Fabrice–Congo

Chandler–USA

Andrew Colum -USA (Oklahoma)

Steve Morabu -Kenya


Jonathan David worked for me for the second time he started near the end of September. Jonathon was 21 had just gotten out of jail again, but I told Jonathan that if he went to jail again before next year to not even ask me for a job next year, because if all I am doing is providing him work between jail stays I didn't feel I was helping him much! He told me he needed to hear that I hope he has changed! Josh Ariel from the family of Juniga as he calls himself came the first week in October, and stayed until we were done with the season. Josh is planning to come back in the spring time to help me with next year's crop. And just as they all came to help one by one they all went in different directions. The first to leave was Bruce he just disappeared no one seems to know where he went! Neighbor David was next he had to finish up with his farming about the time Josh showed up. Ashley Block and Jonathan David were the next to leave as I had no more work for them to do. David Maki left about the first week in November back to the North Country! Jeff was done a few days later. Josh had to stick around a little longer than he planned as we were waiting for the title card for a pickup to come! Joe was the last to leave he has worked here 4 seasons I don't know if I will see him again as he plans to join a religious community in Italy in other words become a monk! Each one leaving leaves a level of sadness within me that I find hard to explain and a void now that I am again by myself. Leaving me to wonder what another season will bring. These were the people next to God who made it possible to have the best year of my farming career!

The Trucks

It is a funny thing that even the pickup trucks that we use to haul the pumpkins develop a personality, one of the trucks we used didn't make it through the season, one just barely did, but with the help of my neighbor mechanic Donny most of them made it to the finish line!

The first one I want to mention is a truck we called Goldie it had been through at least 3 seasons already, this year would have been four, but it was not meant to be. Goldie was a gold straight f150 ford pickup but after being loaded way to heavy too many times it met it demise one Sunday morning out by the Mankato stand I was hauling about 4 barrels of mini pumpkins and was about a mile away when I heard a pounding down by the transmission.

I made it to the stand alright, but only got a mile from there on my return home when it went out totally. David Maki came out and towed me home, and Tom Kennebeck towed me over to Wayne's were it awaits much like other pickups from previous harvest's to be resurrected into a trailer! About this time David made the comment that "at least he hasn't made a trailer out of us yet!" I was thinking on getting another pickup to replace Goldie, but David Scholtz said we could probably get by with the ones we had.

My red f150 that was purchased after the season last year now had to go to work. I had just put on a new set of tires. One day we were all going to have lunch at Uncle Albert's when we got to the Eagle Lake stand. Jeff and Ashley and Jonathon were the only ones to have lunch though, as David Maki almost made it to the stand when a wheel came lose and broke all the stud bolts off! So the rest of us had to keep working so we could get the truck load of gourds off so the tow truck could come before they closed for the day! Thankfully the tire shop paid the bill as they forgot to tell me to re tighten the bolts! The only thing that was hurt was David's pride and the side of the box that the tire had dented in! This truck finished the season with no more problems and was given to Jeff for a bonus at the end of the season! It had been a real blessing to me a year ago and God allowed me to buy something newer this year. I kept my promise that I would not use it this year in the pumpkin field. We did use it at night to collect the money so it became known as the money truck!

Before I started to pick pumpkins this year I asked God for the vehicles he wanted me to have and to have him help me to find them. I found all three on Craig's list Just a few days apart! The first one I found was a red 1992 f250 4x4 ford the biggest in the fleet it came to be known as big red! After a while big red wasn't running to good it smoked a lot and about gaged you to load the thing! First the air conditioning clutch went out we towed it home and a guy we call code red fixed that! Code red's real name is Scott he got the nick name by fixing some wiring in my house he told me that everything in my house was code red so we just started calling him that! The next time it died on the road for Jeff. we had to tow it home unload its load and tow it to Donny's; after a day we got word that it could be fixed, so in a few days we got it back other than a week battery and no tailgate it was practically flawless!

The second pickup I bought was a red 1989 f1504x4 the guy I bought it from knew I was the Hey by George guy! I didn't want to tell him his pickup was a piece of junk so I ended up buying it to save possible damage to my pumpkin stands later on! Terry didn't want me to buy it he said it was cursed! It ran out of gas on me before I got half way home so obviously the gas gage did not work we filled it with gas and found out both tanks leaked one from the bottom and one on the top! We found we could use the trip mile gage to let us know how much gas was in the tank. We could go 100 miles on ten gallons but not 120 as David Scholtz found out one day and had to be towed to the gas station in Cleveland! There probably wasn't a week went by that we didn't have to tow it somewhere! But it did make it through the season with Donny's help and $400! In the end the brakes were pretty bad! Ashley kept the baseball shifting nob for a souvenir and Josh took the radio out. I took off the tail gate and put it on big red. The box was taken off to be exchanged for one that was very poor on one of the trailers! The tires were taken off and the rest was loaded up on a hay wagon with the front end of Goldie and sold for scrap iron I used the proceeds to buy me a new television cabinet for my living room so in the end the curse became a blessing!

Romans 8:28
That's why we can be so sure that every detail in our
lives of love for God is worked into something good.

About the same time I saw the curse on Craig's list I also noticed a blue 1989 f 250 ford it was advertised as only having 53,000 original miles on it! The owner had a list of all the repairs he had done to it but the new tires and aluminum wheels caught my eye! I took

Howard Guse with me down to Pine Island where it was. I checked it out, and bought it for $1350 for an older pickup it was one sweet ride! Other than a transmission seal that cost $600 I had no further trouble with this truck it was one of my most dependable. I gave it the name the blue mule as you could put a load on it plus a trailer load behind and barely felt you had a load! I even drove it down to the Wisconsin Dells church celebration it got 10.5 miles to the gallon and it had one flaw when you braked it liked to pull you to the left. I have been driving these old Fords all my life they are filled with all kinds of quirks and peculiarities! You just have to figure them out! So to drive the blue mule I just braked a little lighter like you were driving on snow and steered slightly to the right I managed just fine. If this pickup would have had 4 wheel drive no one would have gotten it from me, but I gave it to Josh for his bonus and the last I heard it made it to Denver Colorado! That leaves me with big red for my farm truck and my practically new 1994 f 150 4x4 I figure there will be more old ford trucks to be had for next season if there isn't it will be just too bad for me!

The Visitors

Every year I have visitors come just to see for themselves what my pumpkins are all about. Most of them have heard stories of the past and want an experience for themselves, and some have come every year that I can remember they generally make themselves right at home and end up being more of a blessing to me than I am to them! The first visitors to show up was the weekend of September the 15 the pumpkin thing as I call it This is a weekend is devoted to raising money for camps which will be mention in other ministries. I will mention the people who came and some of the things that went on that weekend. On Saturday Tom and Sandy Kennebeck from Orr MN showed up as well as their son Chris who lives in Madelia. They bought with them Lewis Edgel It was his first time here and he enjoyed driving trucks loading and unloading squash as well as entertaining us with the old piano I have in my dining room. Troy Miesner was up from Spring Valley with his son Hunter. Troy also brought Mary porter and Vivian Malcomson. Rick took a picture with those 2 ladies' and me out in the squash field Mary is on my right and Vivian is on my left I am in the center holding a Cinderella pumpkin! Scott and his son Tony were there both from Lakeville MN. Rick Bengston and Steve Deuel from Eastern Wisconsin! 16 loads of large squash were picked and unloaded that day and only one pickup big red clunked out and had to be towed home from Eagle Lake! Early the next morning is when my gold pickup made its last delivery and had to be towed home! Around noon The Gjesvold family, and Travis and Sheila Muellner showed up as well as Charles Holladay, Mike and Daniel Haack, Doug and Betty Johannsen. We were picking small squash that day. As we were picking Mike came across a big stone I had unearthed while cultivating earlier in the season. I was always going to go back there with my skid loader and pick it up, and forgotten about it until now. Mike asked if he could have it, sure I said. We Got Doug to bring his pickup over and Mike and his brother picked the big stone up and put it in Doug's pickup! It taught me that God will remove our obstacles if we are patient, even if he has to provide a couple of Giants to do it! Just a while later Charles was driving one of the pickups Daniel was in back holding on to garbage cans full of squash while Mike and I were loading them. We were on a pretty steep hill 2 barrels full of squash came rolling back out of the truck and spilled on the ground. Mike hollered at Dan to hold onto the barrels as they were all starting to come back out. "Jeepers Creepers" was all Dan said back to Mike. It was one of those times you really had to be there to appreciate the seen; it was so funny I fell to my knees in laughter!

My sister Marie was here for about 10 days from Redmond Oregon. I was so busy while she was here that I told her if she wanted to visit with me she would have to work with me throughout the day, so she did! Marie worked all afternoon with us picking mini pumpkins, and when evening came she went on the run with me. Marie said it just amazed her about the size of my business and how it all worked she said she didn't know anything like it which doesn't surprise me because I really didn't copy anyone it is a unique creation! Dad and I plan to fly out to Oregon to visit Marie in February so hopefully we will have a more normal visit! The first week in October My cousins from Illinois were here Donna, Nancy, and Kyla. Brad and Kelly were also here for the weekend from Oklahoma. Troy Peterson stopped by to visit with Brad while he was here. 2 evenings in a row Kyla sang for us before her Nancy and myself would go on the run with me during this time we had loads of fun! Tom and Sandy Kennebeck were also back down from Orr on that Saturday as the school paid them to come back and get some more pumpkins! I wanted to show my cousins the pumpkin farm before they drove back to Illinois. When we got over there it was like something in explicable was happening! Steve and the Kenyan's were out there picking. Wayne my Land lord was helping them. My cousins were there from Illinois, as well as Brad from Oklahoma, and it came to me that Right out in the pumpkin field we had Land Lord, Worker, and tenant all working side by side. We had people from different countries as well as 4 different states out there and it seemed for a moment in time things were the way they were supposed to be! Tom, Wayne, Steve, and I said a prayer for protection for the pumpkins as that evening the temps were supposed to get down to 19 degrees that evening. Pictures were taken of us all; Kyla calls them the "Amazing Hallelujah!"

Sometime in here we had a couple visitors come to the home stand. A lady from St. Peter introduced these folks as her relatives from Sweden. Jeff was telling me that maybe it was the King and Queen! I had no Idea what he was getting at. Later that day I was over to Smiths Mill implement to get some parts I was telling someone over there that I even had some visitors from Sweden that day at my home stand. Rick said it was probably the King and Queen of Sweden as they were visiting Gustavas Adolfus collage in St. Peter at that time! You could have knocked me down with a feather at this point here I could have had the King and Queen of Sweden here and I didn't even know it! At very least they were part of their entourage! Latter on it was discovered that indeed it was the King and Queen of Sweden If I would have only known! I would have talked to them more instead of being so concerned of my work!

Proverbs 22:29
Do you see a man who excels in his work? He will stand before kings; He will not stand before unknown men.

Jordan Porter Drove up from southern Wisconsin the second weekend in October I was glad He got to meet Steve and the Kenyan's as it was the last day that they worked for me. One morning I woke

Jordan at 5 am as we had to haul a load of pumpkins down to Mike Haacks a hundred miles east of here! Josh, Jordan, and I also hauled a load up to Scott's that day in Lakeville. Jordan showed me a way to sort the money on the run that was better than the way I was doing it so I used his technique for the rest of the season! Everyone seems to add a little to all of this in some way! I asked Jordan what he thought about my business while he was here he said it sure testifies to the amount of faith that I have. I don't know why I always find that statement amusing as I heard it several times this year! Before Jordan Left he got to pick out a thanksgiving turkey from Joe's flock! Jordan was here until 10 am Sunday morning Josh and I said good bye to him from the Eagle Lake stand. Jordan said he had the time of his life the few days he was here. I am sure it was a unique experience!

One day Paul Schwartz stopped me out on the road near the pumpkins I had heard he was home for a while from the military. It was good to see Paul again 'and I could see that the military was good for him he seems more polished! Paul helped us out with about 8 loads of pumpkins and I bought his dinner and he ate with us. Paul would be returning soon to camp Pendleton in San Diego. I couldn't help crying when I hugged him good by seems like I'm doing that more as the years go by. Some say that I am just getting soft maybe they are right?

Denise Olson and grandsons Michael and Gabriel from Juneau Wisconsin came on the weekend of October 20. Denise had asked me if it was alright to bring along her dogs sure I said! We were starting to slow down with the pumpkins they had all been picked and put in rows by the Kenyan's they were no longer coming, but I still needed help putting them out by the stands so there were still plenty of pumpkins to be picked up. I had to go to a wedding Saturday afternoon so

Josh had to entertain every one while I was gone! Denise was able to come on the run with me to see most of the stands. She made the same comment as my sister Marie did that she was just amazed by it all! Denise is my sister in Christ, and she was glad that Michael and Gabriel could have such an experience!

Miss Britta Anne Lahr from Eau Claire Wisconsin was our final visitor for the season. Though she didn't come to work with the pumpkins she came to paint a couple rooms for me! Britta mentioned to me in an email that one of her hobbies were painting and decorating. I mentioned that I had a couple of rooms I was redoing that needed to be painted so I asked her if she would be willing to come up and paint them for me. Britta said she would if she could get some time off this fall. I know it was a God thing that she came, because it didn't look like she was going to make it any more this year. We had slowed down quite a bit with the pumpkins I wanted to get the carpets put in before Joe left for good as he was the only one I knew who would tackle the job! I was just about ready to send Joe and Josh to get some carpeting, when I heard from Britta wondering if it would work for her to come down that weekend to paint! Perfect timing I would say! I let Britta pick out the paint and the carpeting, because believe me decorating isn't my forte! Two rooms were a pretty big job for only 2 days to do the work. After a while I could see that Josh needed to help Britta if she was going to get this project done. They got far enough along so it was safe to let Josh and Joe finish up the rooms! Now I can say that after 3 years the whole first level of my house has been redone! Many thanks Britta the rooms turned out great, and I can't help but think of the wonderful weekend we all had every time I step into my living room! Twice Britta came on the run with me. The first night Britta took care of the money, and the second night she drove the pickup! One of the nights we had to stop at Menards to get some stuff for the rooms. We left $3000 on the seat of the pickup in a 5 gallon pail I locked my door and assumed Britta had locked her door, but when we came out Britta's door was not locked! How I know this is my key won't work on the driver's side it only will unlock the passenger door! We had a good laugh as nothing was lost! The next evening I let Britta drive and I took care of the money. We put a pumpkin in the oven, because Britta wanted to make a pumpkin pie while she was here. I thought it would save time if we baked the pumpkin while we were gone instead of when we got back. David, Joe, and Josh were covering up the squash that evening to prevent it from freezing. So Josh picked up some ingredients and pie crust while they were going through town. Britta texted her sister Heather that she was driving my pickup. When we got home and after we took care of the money, the guys showed up and the pumpkin was done baking. They were looking for pie pans to bake the pie in, but I had none. I suggested that we put the 2 pie crusts over the bottom of my cast iron fry pan it would hold all the ingredients and we would have one huge pie! After that was done the pie had to bake, but at 1o'clock that morning we had one of the best pumpkin pies ever! When I think back on that weekend it reminds me of a chapter from a Pippi Longstocking Book! Thank you so much for coming Britta, what a grand adventure is all I can say!

Other Ministries

In the last couple of years I have started to notice how other ministries are starting to rest so to speak in the branches of mine referring to the scripture I have used to start this story out. Here are a few I know of.

Tom and Sandy Kennebeck come down from Orr Minnesota every year they always take a load of pumpkins back with them to sell to provide the youth with money to go to camps and do other things.

Another Pastor I know gleaned my squash fields and picked up some of the deer bitten ones that would not sell on my stands. He took out the good parts of them and gave them to some people he knows and works with.

Various churches and organizations get pumpkins every year most of these are donated by me. I find I can help them way more that way, then if they were asking for a monetary gift!

Several youth camps are affected by the pumpkins that are grown.

The Maranatha ministries from the collage in Mankato are now affected via Steve and the Kenyan's.

Several head start programs from various towns use the pumpkin stands for their field trips with no cost to them.

Two churches allow me to sell pumpkins on their grounds.

These are just some of the ministries that I am aware of!

The Future

One of the most noticed things for me I sense as I finish with the plowing for the year. Is that there seems to be a great peace that has settled over the land! No more do I feel what is like static electricity within and without myself at all times! Perhaps the peace was always there covered up by the day to day happenings to produce this crop! No more are the times I wonder about the weather, the bugs, and the diseases. For those prayers have all been answered! To survive not having any land at first to grow them on. Then a hail storm, drought, vine disease, bug infestation, and 2 nights below 20 degrees, and end up with an increase of 46% growth from the previous year is nothing short of miraculous to me! I give God all the glory for this as it certainly wasn't anything I had done! If I am still around come springtime I recon God willing I will do it all again, but if Jesus returns I am out of here, because I am truly looking forward to seeing THE land I can finally call home!

1John 2:12-17

12 I remind you, my dear children: Your sins are forgiven in Jesus' name. 13 You veterans were in on the ground floor, and know the One who started all this; you newcomers have won a big victory over the Evil One. 14 You veterans know the One who started it all; and you newcomers–such vitality and strength! God's word is so steady in you. Your fellowship with God enables you to gain a victory over the Evil One. 15 Don't love the world's ways. Don't love the world's goods. Love of the world squeezes out love for the Father. 16 Practically everything that goes on in the world–wanting your own way, wanting everything for yourself, wanting to appear important–has nothing to do with the Father. It just isolates you from him. 17 The world and all it's wanting, wanting, wanting is on the way out–but whoever does what God wants is set for eternity.

God's blessings and peace to you all!
In Christ,
George Denn

# Hey By George! February 25- 26 2013

# A MAN'S ACTIONS FOLLOW HIS BELIEFS

Philippians 3:12-16

12 I'm not saying that I have this all together, that I have it made. But I am well on my way, reaching out for Christ, who has so wondrously reached out for me. 13 Friends, don't get me wrong: By no means do I count myself an expert in all of this, but I've got my eye on the goal, where God is beckoning us onward–to Jesus. 14 I'm off and running, and I'm not turning back. 15 So let's keep focused on that goal, those of us who want everything God has for us. If any of you have something else in mind, something less than total commitment, God will clear your blurred vision–you'll see it yet! 16 Now that we're on the right track, let's stay on it.

"A man's actions follow his belief." That was one of the nuggets I got out of Anthony Mullins talk about listening to the Holy Spirit during his first session at Saturdays camp training retreat.

I was sort of surprised as I've used that very phrase a lot over the past 17.5 years of my life! I have 3 books published and 4 stories on how I do this in my own life. Nowadays most people I know put great store in the college degrees that they hold or are working towards, and rightly so I would be the last person to snub a higher education, because sometimes not having one leaves me feeling inept at times, but since following Jesus is done by the heart the only degree one really needs is the one I have 98.6! Some of the writers of the bible had no more credentials than that! And like me I am sure they had to work with 110 degrees as well as–30 degrees! Ok so much for my humor today. I am once again eagerly awaiting springtime to arrive. To drive away the snow that we have, as well as my seasonal depression, because for me winter time is getting to be long! My seasonal depression sets in somewhere about our first snowfall and doesn't leave until the first 60 degree day in the springtime. To live with this condition I try to get my work done by mid-November, and try to do as little as possible until springtime comes. The first 6 weeks of not having anything to do is kind of welcome, but as winter lingers on I get bored with nothing to do and long for springtime to come! To combat boredom I go visiting people. This past Thanksgiving I took a load of wood, and some hay down to Ray and Denise Olson's near Juneau Wisconsin. One of the highlights for me was visiting with Ky for an Hour and to give him the gift I had for him, that I had been keeping since September! After that I drove down to Pewaukee Wisconsin to visit Tracy and Cheri Porter and family. Stephan and Lilly Hill, Sarah and Chris Phelps, and Rick Bengtson were also there everyone had a good time. I was one

Of the last ones to leave. I didn't know it at the time, but I had left my winter coat on a chair. Tracy told Rick sometime later that when I had left He had run beside me hollering and trying to get my attention, but I just drove away oblivious to anything at all. I must have been lost in thought as that sort of thing has happened before. The picture I have in my mind of this is somewhat humorous though! Just days before Christmas, I drove up to Gordy Lindquist's near Duluth, from there further still up to Orr MN. I didn't let anyone know I was coming so when I walked into church up there Tom Kennebeck for one was greatly surprised! And a great church service was had by all! The next day I drove back down to Gordy's. I had it in mind to leave for home I didn't want to impose on anyone's Christmas, but Bonnie convinced me I should stay pointing out that I really didn't have anything to go home for anyway! So stay I did, we all went to a movie that afternoon and went to the timber lodge for the evening meal. That evening as gift were handed out I really didn't expect anything, but I got a small can of almonds and a pocket flashlight! The next day we went to Carroll Millers for Christmas dinner, and I was finally able to get him the bag of wheat that he had asked me for last June! Towards the end of January Snow Blast was held at a Boy Scout camp near Eveleth MN. So Back up to the North Country I went! The second morning we were there it was so cold that the fire place wouldn't draw and I smoked up the whole room; there were about 50 people present for the event. The last morning we were there it was somewhere between 25- 30 below -0 for a temp. Since I had bought my pickup last fall, and we had such a mild winter up to this point, I had failed to winterize the thing even knowing it had come from Arizona! Well it all caught up with me, and proved to be the only vehicle that wouldn't start. It took sometime even after prayer for Tom, Floyd, Doug, and I to get the thing running! I was telling Doug that my life was always this way! Either my vehicle is the only one to start, or the only one that doesn't start! On the 6th of February dad and I flew out to see my sister Marie who lives in Terrebonne Oregon. This means "good soil" in French. I sort of wonder about the French guy who named it this as all I see is dessert and mountains and if you want to grow things out there it has to be Irrigated! I guess if you like that sort of thing there is beauty in the ruggedness, but give me Minnesota anytime where God waters the crops so I don't have too! I did appreciate my brother in law Les's hot tub that he had outside. It was kind of strange sitting in the thing being warmed by the flowing water while my hair on my head was starting to get frosty! For some reason before I went out to Oregon I was apprehensive about going, but once I got out there I was glad to have went which seems strange as usually I am excited to travel? One of the things I did while I was out there was to re-read everything I had ever written up to this point in time. This helped to encourage me as well as to see that God has really expanded my life in the 11 years that I have been writing stories. Everything that I have gone through in past 17.5 years is a result of my actions following my belief in Jesus Christ and listening to what the Holy Spirit was telling me to do. After I had returned home from Oregon a man stopped out and bought the last of the hay I had for sale he was telling me that he knew quite a few people that drive a long way to get pumpkins from me. He also made the statement that once they come here for them they wouldn't want to go anywhere else! "What's up with the book?" he asked. I mentioned there were actually three of them now. "They are stories about my walk with the Lord." I said. He mentioned that I probably do a lot of writing during the winter. "Not really." I said. "As a matter of fact I couldn't write a thing that day to save my life; I had to be inspired to do it!" The last story I wrote was in November and had no idea I would be writing this one! And who knows if I will ever be inspired to write another? I gave him a copy of the books before he left. As a matter of fact it kind of offends me when people try to buy them; I just would rather give them away! Dad and I left for Illinois on the 21st I wanted to get down there before the snowstorm of the century hit! Next morning there was only an inch of snow, so much for the snowstorm of the century! That day I watched a commentary at Cousin Nancy's place on how the swamps in the Kankakee River basin had been drained 150 years ago and the old timer's that had drained them. I often think of how hard those old people's lives were to form this great country, and how easy most of us have life today. How often do we give them a thought; if ever, while we are working at our computers, or on our degrees. If it wasn't for those hard working people of long ago; would any of this ease of life as we know it be possible for us today? NOT! Friday afternoon I drove the 110 miles from Nancy's house to the camp. Every time I enter that place there is always a sense of excitement and anticipation. It is always good to see people of like mind that you haven't seen in a while. The first three people I saw was Jim Barnhill caretaker of the camp, Stephan Hill, and Chris Phelps care taker of the food! Shortly thereafter many more arrived. I think we all retired for the night around 11 PM. After breakfast the next morning we were guided throughout the day by Anthony Mullins or "White Gravy" as Nathan Keating calls him! I had to ask Anthony about this white gravy stuff! Evidently down in Texas they pour this white gravy on their food. Anthony likes this white gravy and really uses a lot of it, so Nathan calls Anthony "white gravy" because of this. Since I've never been to Texas except for being at an airport; I really don't know what the heck they are talking about, so I came up with my own nickname for Anthony, something I will re-veil later on in this story! Anthony mentioned to me that he would be watching me to see if I fell asleep while he was talking! This is something that amuses a lot of people especially those who hold some sort of degree in theology. James Newby last fall at the Dells celebration referred to me during the start of his message, as the guy everyone knows that falls asleep during church! Which by the sound of the laughter amused many? This never bothers me though, as I too often wonder why I do this. It usually is never because the speaker is boring, this too was re-veiled to me by the Holy Spirit just 3 days ago why I do this and I will re-veil it before the end of this story! We had several breakout sessions during the day. Bob Shippits, Tony Raney, Dave Holmes, and Rick Bengston were in my group. We were supposed to tell each person how we saw God at work in their life and at camp. One common denominator amongst the guys were that each person did not think as highly of themselves as the rest of the guys viewed them, which was a good sign of humility something I feel I rarely poses! After lunch we had some more words from Anthony, and then he divided us up into six groups. I forgot most of the questions he asked I think there were 6 of them. The one I do remember was if you could have the ultimate job at camp what would that be? I re-member my times down in the dorms which were very rewarding, but also the most taxing! I did and always will feel that the role of the councilor is the most important, and when I was in that role I didn't take it lightly, but am also glad to be retired from that position! Several times at different camps I found myself teaching a class, but feel teaching a group is not one of my strong points, although I do seem to do well on a one on one situation. I thought I already have the ultimate role at camp being on the security team. I have been there so long that I can pretty much tell what needs to be done. I was also somewhat amused to find out that on three other Teams, what George does was their Idea of the ultimate Job! I have lived 50 years on this earth and during that time I came up with this phrase I use quite a bit probably from personal experience; "Be careful what you want, you might get it!" Security can be a very easy Job, but it can also be a very demanding job you have to be ready in a moment's notice to do just about anything. We may be called upon to assist others when campers get out of control I have seen this more than once. If there would be a tornado or something we are not the first people to get to safety! I know seeing us ride around on Gators and golf carts may look glamorous, but they are intended to get us around fast and we take people where they need to be, and sometimes prevent people where they want to be! None the less I feel this is the ultimate position, and this stage of my life it fits me like a glove. Later that evening, after supper like many years at these retreats. A group game of what Dave Holmes calls the 7 of hearts was shaping up! I took a place at the end of the table. James Shunkwiler and Britta Lahr were to my right. Rick Bengston and Big Al and a few people down stood Anthony Mullins to my left! During the course of the game Anthony was acting differently than a man that holds the degree he does would be expected to act! I on the other hand not having much better luck, and being the 98.6 degrees that I am, I asked Anthony what age he was. "42" was Anthony's answer. Right at that moment was when I knew The Holy Spirit let me know I had a story to write, and I told Anthony so. Britta Lahr told Anthony to be careful around George you may end up in one of his stories, but the warning came too late! I just want to take some space to mention here that over the years I have wrote about a lot of people that for some reason or

71

another God has put in my life. I am of the belief that there is some reason that you know the people you know they are not in your life by chance. I have tried very hard not to offend anyone by what I have written, but at the same time inject some humor into the situation. This is probably because since day 1 that I noticed God at work in my life, generally humor was not far behind! So if I have ever written anything that has offended any one for this I am truly sorry, but you will have to take that one up with God as he was the one who wants me to write them, because I have quit twice already! Time to re-veil Anthony's nick name that I have given him. I will call him "The 7 of hearts" from now on. And Anthony like any good card player knows you can only play the hand to which you were dealt! That evening story after story was told about former camps and different stories throughout our lives. Some of us laughed until we cried remembering them all! After breakfast the next morning there was nothing left to do but say good bye to those who had stayed overnight. I declare! What friends God has given me over the years! And to think 17.5 years ago I left all the friends that I had at the time except one. And walked forward into the fellowship we are all now a part of! WOW! It is always anything but easy to say good bye to this group of people, and afterward I drove the 110 miles back to Cousin Nancy's place to get some rest and pick up Dad so we could come back to Minnesota the following day. That evening while I was lying in bed I was thinking back over my life. Born third child with 4 siblings to parents that only had an 8th grade education. They were farmers for the most part, but also had jobs away from there. I live in the same house I have for all these 50 years that this story is written in. God didn't allow me to be with the person I wanted to spend my life with. I often pray for her and see how God used her in my life to break my heart and get me on a different path, but at the same time am very glad I did not end up with that person! I also had to walk away from every friend I had at the time, because I knew if I didn't I would never get to where God wanted me to be. I also walked away from the Catholic Church I grew up in. Out of one world and into another so to speak into an obscure church that had been shook to its very core by a series of doctrinal changes I even remember the day June 17 1995. I didn't know a soul the day I walked through the doors but was stopped dead by the presents of God. Later that year there was only about 20 people left, and I wondered why I didn't leave myself, it was because I didn't have any were else to go, so I might just as well stay and see what happens, as I had walked away from everyone and anything I had ever known. In that little group as time went on I was called upon to lead worship and give messages every once in a while. One day Darlene Woods asked me if I would write something every once in a while for a church newsletter and Hey by George! Was born. I didn't want to see it close I was one of the few that voted to keep it open, but close it did 8 years ago. I stay true to the fellowship God called me into through the youth camps that I've been involved with and friendships I have cultivated these past 17.5 years. I went through bankruptcy 11 years ago and had to watch all that I had ever worked for get hauled away. Two years ago I got my home farm taken away and had to watch others farm this place that I had known as home for 49 years. God replaced that with a different farm better in every way than this one was. It was through that experience that God showed me that I was not in charge of my own provision that he was, because for the last 2 years I actually made something doing this, but I give God the glory, because I'm not doing anything different than I ever did! God Showed me that night in bed that this year my farm touched the lives of nearly 50,000 people; with the Pumpkins I raise and the stories I have written. I was reminded at this time of the plaque my aunt gave me as a gift for my High school Graduation. I didn't care for it much back then, but have come to appreciate it now, and I just hung it up over my bedroom door yesterday! It reads as follows.

### George
"INDUSTRIOUS"
Trust in the Lord, and do good;
so shalt thou dwell in the land, and
verily thou shalt be fed.
Psalm 37:3

Steve Marabu my friend from Kenya Africa made a statement to me last fall while we were working with the pumpkins one day. He said that "I can see that God has taken you far!" I too this late winter day can see how far God has taken me! And that's the reason why I fall asleep like I do. Here God has put me in charge of this mega ministry and I hadn't even realized it! True, I have had many a hired man over the years; and I think of everyone with fondness, nor can there help be discounted. But Jesus did have something to say about hired men that I find interesting.

John 10:11-15
11 "I am the Good Shepherd. The Good Shepherd puts the sheep before himself, sacrifices himself if necessary. 12 A hired man is not a real shepherd. The sheep mean nothing to him. He sees a wolf come and

runs for it, leaving the sheep to be ravaged and scattered by the wolf. 13 He's only in it for the money. The sheep don't matter to him. 14 "I am the Good Shepherd. I know my own sheep and my own sheep know me. 15 In the same way, the Father knows me and I know the Father. I put the sheep before myself, sacrificing myself if necessary.

So the next time you see me fall asleep while your speaking or at church laugh if you must; and know I will probably laugh with you! But also say a prayer for me that God would send this unique person into my life to help me with this unique ministry that he has given me!

Genesis 8:21-23
21 God put the Man into a deep sleep. As he slept he removed one of his ribs and replaced it with flesh. 22 God then used the rib that he had taken from the Man to make Woman and presented her to the Man. 23 The Man said, "Finally! Bone of my bone, flesh of my flesh! Name her Woman for she was made from Man."

In closing I hope my Evangelical friends will forgive me if I revisit my Catholic past to a scripture that meant a lot to me at the beginning of my walk with Jesus, because I have thought of it a lot over the years! Some where I have heard that a man's actions should follow his beliefs.

Sirach 7:15

Hate not laborious tasks, nor farming which was ordained by the Most High.

If that is true it really humbles me, because my credentials were given to me from the one that holds the Highest Degree!

Gods' peace and blessings to you all!

In Christ

George Denn

# Hey By George! March 31 2013

# FRIENDS OLD AND NEW HITHER AND YON

Part 1 the adventure begins!

> Proverbs 18:24
> A man who has friends must himself be friendly, But
> there is a friend who sticks closer than a brother.

It was Pastor Todd Fox that the Holy Spirit spoke to me through this morning at Rochester MN Grace Communion Church! I was there celebrating resurrection Sunday with my friends at that fellowship. Todd said one of the things that he enjoyed about the day was that he was able to celebrate the day with his friends! I was thinking back to where my journey started, Wednesday March 20 the first day of spring! I had invited David Maki and Wayne Schwartz to watch the passion of the Christ movie with me that evening. Wayne told me he had never seen it yet, he said he was always afraid too! I was telling Wayne that it was high time that he had. We each had a glass of Mogan David wine, ok I had two! On its label it says kosher for the Passover. Since Jesus is our Passover lamb I didn't figure that he would mind that!

1 Corinthians 5:7-8
So get rid of this "yeast." Our true identity is flat and plain, not puffed up with the wrong kind of ingredient. The Messiah, our Passover Lamb, has already been sacrificed for the Passover meal, and we are the Unraised Bread part of the Feast. 8 So let's live out our part in the Feast, not as raised bread swollen with the yeast of evil, but as flat bread–simple, genuine, unpretentious.

Every time I watch that show I come away with something different. This time I noticed that the guards just would not stop whipping or kicking Jesus until he was attached to the cross and lifted up. It always amuses me how quickly his tormentors react once they realize what they had done!

Matthew 27:50-54
But Jesus, again crying out loudly, breathed his last. 51 At that moment, the Temple curtain was ripped in two, top to bottom. There was an earthquake, and rocks were split in pieces. 52 What's more, tombs were opened up, and many bodies of believers asleep in their graves were raised. 53 (After Jesus' resurrection, they left the tombs, entered the holy city, and appeared to many.) 54 The captain of the guard and those with him, when they saw the earthquake and

everything else that was happening, were scared to death. They said, "This has to be the Son of God!"

The end of the movie is my favorite and most important part I think. Jesus just gets up and walks right out of the tomb! Just as alive as you or I! A guy had called me about a load of firewood, just before we had watched the movie. I really am not in the firewood business anymore and I felt like telling him so, but I did have about 10 loads yet I would sell if anyone would call. I have delivered to this fellow before he is crippled and always wants his wood stacked on his deck behind his house and up a stairs so it is convenient for him to get to! But it is very inconvenient for me and hardly worth the effort as it has to be carried a long ways, and by myself it's like the wood sale from hell! David and Wayne both said they would go with me, and after watching the movie I was mad at myself for thinking the way I did about this person after all, had not God blessed me with this person in the past for my provision in the years that I needed it? I made up my mind that we would do whatever it took to make it as convenient as we could for him to retrieve his wood! Wayne showed up the next morning and all three of us went with the load of wood. I was happy to have the help and not have to do this myself! First thing that happened all three of us got out of the truck, but one of us hit the locking device on the door. There we were 20 miles from home where an extra set of keys were, and with the engine running! I told the guys my friend Doug Johannsen's famous line "no good deed goes unpunished!" And we all laughed! While David and Wayne worked on getting the door unlocked I started carrying wood. They had success and I was able to back the truck closer to where we were stacking the wood. The man was surprised that I had changed my mind and stacked his wood where he originally wanted it stacked. I told him that was alright, but that he needed to understand that after this I am out of the firewood business. Wayne said that it did us all good to do that for the man, and we all agreed. I have come to know Wayne Swartz through a sale of organic hay probably about 7 years ago now. I was getting ready to leave the next morning; my friend Tracy Porter from Pewaukee Wisconsin had this piece of land down in South Carolina that he wanted me to look at. We had been throwing the idea around for a couple of years now and almost went last January, but Jordan had to have an operation that prevented him from going at that time! The plan was that I would drive down that Friday, and after Church on Saturday, Jordan Tracy and I would head east. I already knew this would be an adventure so I kept my eyes and ears open for what God had in store! I left here on Friday morning around 9 am. I had no time restraints to get there nor when to get home. The way things looked around here I wouldn't be doing any field work until April sometime anyway! I find it is always more interesting to be operating on Gods time kairos, then our time chronos. As you never know what may be in store for you! I got down to the Porter's about 4 pm Joseph was there as well as Tracy to greet me. Jordan showed up shortly after that starting his spring break from collage and Cherie showed up shortly after Jordan from her work. This family I have come to know from working at heartland youth summer camp near Peoria IL. and the Wisconsin dells fall celebration over the years probably all of nine by now. It came out during a time of prayer with this family that I remember a time when I did not know this family, but I could hardly imagine what it would be like not to have this family be a part of my life now! The plan on Saturday was that Tracy and Cherie would go to church early to help set up for the

Chile dinner that was to follow services. I would ride with Jordan and Joseph. We were five minutes late so Joseph and I decided we would just point at Jordan if everyone turned and looked at us when we walked in! But Jordan left us off at the door and snuck in after us no one even heard us come in! Chris and Sarah Phelps were the first ones I saw and you could tell by their faces that they were either amused or happy to see us, maybe both? I have known Sarah for 9 years we both worked together the first year at camp in outdoor activities and we both have more stories from that year to fill a book! She and I didn't always see eye to eye that year, but I have come to appreciate Sarah as one of my sisters in the Lord! Her husband Chris, I have come to know these past few years I see he definitely has the gift of hospitality, and is well liked as well as greatly appreciated as he is our camps cook! Danielle Lahr had just come back from her mission trip in Cambodia. She had gone over there last year in May sometime I think? Danielle went there to serve and tell about Jesus to women and children who were involved in the sex trafficking industry in that country. Tracy Porter is the pastor of the church where Danielle was asked to talk of her experiences. Tracy asked Danielle a series of questions of her experience in Cambodia. Tracy asked her a question I forget exactly what was asked, but it was about evangelism. My interpretation of her answer is that you really have to know a person well before you will have much success with it. That's my interpretation of her answer and my experience with it as well. I have forgotten most of the questions and answers at this point, but I remember something she said I could relate to. I could relate to what she said by sometimes she just had to give things to God to work out because if she tried to force things they would not turn out well! As a farmer I should know this by looking at the crops. What crop does not produce fruit easily as well as naturally? I got the opportunity to visit with Danielle a little more at lunchtime and greatly appreciated the opportunity. Although Danielle has been a part of heartland camp for some time I do not know her well, but view it as a God thing that I know her at all. And look forward to get to know her better as time goes on. Britta Lahr was there I was surprised to see her as I didn't think I would see her until the end of July! I met Britta a few years back at heartland camp. We had a shoot-out with each other during paintball and I lost. I've never held it against her though, and we have been friends since. Britta introduced me to her mother before lunch and we had a great talk. I was rather amused when she told me her husband Monty Lahr had used some of my stories I have written as a teaching for his small group! I was hoping to visit with him that day, because I had met him last fall, but other than a quick hand shake and hi it was not meant to be. Latter after lunch I stopped to talk with Britta and Danielle and Mrs. Lahr at their table Jordan and Joseph Porter was also there visiting. We were talking about things that went on at camp, and about some of the things that went on up here last fall while Britta was here. Mrs. Lahr asked me if I knew her other daughter Heather and her son Micah. I told her that I really didn't know Heather I could tell you who she was by being at camp, the same goes for Micah, but I've never talked with ether of them. People were starting to leave so I went upstairs to get my coat so I would be ready when Tracy and Jordan were ready to go. I was looking at the pictures Danielle took over in Cambodia from what I seen Danielle must have had quite the experience there. I asked Britta what she thought of the yummy bowl of snakes that was at a market place. She said she just turns the page when she gets to that picture! I am undecided which would be a worse fate to sit down to a meal of snakes in Cambodia or a plate full of mud cookies in Haiti? Hopefully I will never have to find out! But after looking at Danielle's pictures all Americans should be very thankful for what they have! Again just before they left I got into a conversation with Mrs. Lahr. I asked her what her name was as I am always interested in people's names usually a person lives up to what their name means! She said her name was Dace, I thought it unique as I have never heard it before. I asked her if she knew what it meant "no" she said she didn't. I was kidding her when I said well that's the project for the week to find out what your name means! As far as I can tell Dace means- of the south- or of the nobility! It was fun visiting with the Lahr's they are a unique family, and I mean that in a good way!

I had a thought while I was writing this story and didn't quite know where to place it so for no other reason I will put it here at the end of part one I hope it is fitting. I have come to know a lot of people far younger than myself. I have also come to know a lot of people far older than myself. Growing up I seemed to want to hang around the older folks their lives and story's seemed to be more colorful than those of my age how they thought and what they thought of seemed to make more sense to me than those of my own age, and I didn't always agree with what those my age were getting themselves into! Therefore I tend to understand my older friends better than my younger ones. I don't think Jesus intended for us to spend our time with just those of our age. Jesus was a friend of all, and young and old followed him. I don't think Jesus much likes the generation Gap that has gotten bigger since world war 2 before that young and old practically Dressed the same, thought the same, and pretty much had much of the same music oh there were some differences that is only natural, but not like today our world we live in seems to have done this to us. If Jesus returned what age group would he like to be with? I think he would like to be with them all. I recall when I was 14 my best friend at the time was 77 years old and lived across the road from us, and I enjoyed our friendship immensely! I would not know some of the things I know today if it wasn't for Martin and his wife Hattie. What dear friends they were, they were killed in a car wreck in 1986; I was 24 at the time. I haven't a doubt in my mind that I will see them again when we are all resurrected!

> Revelation 20:11-15
> I saw a Great White Throne and the One Enthroned.
> Nothing could stand before or against the Presence,
> nothing in Heaven, nothing on earth. 12 And then I saw
> all the dead, great and small, standing there–before the
> Throne! And books were opened. Then another book
> was opened: the Book of Life. The dead were judged
> by what was written in the books, by the way they had
> lived. 13 Sea released its dead, Death and Hell turned
> in their dead. Each man and woman was judged by the
> way he or she had lived. 14 Then Death and Hell were
> hurled into Lake Fire. This is the second death–Lake
> Fire. 15 Anyone whose name was not found inscribed
> in the Book of Life was hurled into Lake Fire.

I just want to say to my younger friends who are younger than I that may be reading this that I may not always understand you, but I value your friendships deeply!

Part 2 The Journey

Jordan, Tracy, and I were all loaded up and ready to go as soon as we were done at church. Our destination, Bluefield Virginia from my place here that's 1050 miles like they say down South "that's a right fer piece!" We were not too far into Ohio when Tracy mentioned that we would be going right by where Amy Gould lived and if possible we should look her up. For quite a few years Amy Gould was our camp cook down at Heartland! Which bought up the topic of me putting a sack of hornets in the freezer! I don't think she ever quite got over that one! Tracy did get in touch with Amy, but it wouldn't work out for her to meet us this evening; We would try again on our return trip! We were looking for a Cracker Barrel restaurant, but because it was dark it was hard to spot one! On our return trip they were all over the place we couldn't see the signs because of the darkness. Finally we found one, after that Jordan drove the rest of the way. I slept mostly, but when I woke up after a while you could see the mountains all dark and tall all around us. We arrived in Bluefield Virginia around 3 am, and were greeted by Tracy's Mother Gerrie. When we got up the next morning everything was covered in snow! I got the feeling it was following me around! I enjoyed viewing the mountains from the windows of the warm house. For some reason I feel right at home here in these mountains. I can't say that about the ones out in Oregon. So for some reason mountains must not be all the same, perhaps it's the familiar hard wood trees that grow on these mountains as well as back home? I could tell right off that Gerrie's Gifts of the Holy Spirit were Hospitality and giving. Gerrie is a care giver to her husband Howard. He had a stroke some years back and is no longer able to take care of himself. These folks remind me of my Mom and

Dad; my Father was a caregiver to my Mother. Gerrie was a wealth of information of their family history! If I have my facts straight the land that Tracy's dad gave him has been in his family for 222 years since 1791! According to Howard it had been sold off about 3 times over the years. The Native people to this part of the country is English or Scotch. Which makes sense as England owned this area before the revolutionary war. Tracy said the first Porter from his family can be traced as coming from England to Lancaster co. Virginia sometime in the 1600's. That first afternoon the snow had turned to rain so Tracy took us first to see his aunt Agnes. Agnes is 90 years old and her bible is full of names and dates! She told Tracy to find a spot to write Jordan and Joseph's names and birth dates in which looked like no easy task, but he eventually found a spot! After our visit with Agnes, Tracy took us to the cemetery were his grandma and grandpa Kidd, Gerrie's mother and father were buried. They were way up on a side hill, but it quit raining long enough for us to walk up there and get back. The graves were mostly all decorated with flowers for Easter it really was a beautiful place! After that Tracy took us around and showed us the different places they had lived while he was growing up the school he went to seemed small compared to the one I went to, but Bluefield only has about a 5000 population. So like a lot of us I could see that Tracy started in pretty humble beginnings! That evening, after more food and conversation Jordan wanted to watch some zombie apocalypse show on TV. The older folks didn't much care for the show so they retired for the evening. I'm not much for monsters and scare type movies ether, but neither was I ready for bed yet so I watched the show with Jordan. Let's just say the movie didn't do much for me! The next morning everything was covered in snow again! The plan for the day was to drive down to South Carolina a three hour drive.

We left a snowy Virginia and arrived in South Carolina where the red bud trees were budding, people were mowing their lawns for the first time, and the dogwood trees are in bloom! There is a legend down south that Jesus was crucified on a dogwood tree. That's why it grows so short and spindly because it was cursed ever since! Personally I don't think legends are all what they are cracked up to be! Supposedly here where I live I am somewhat of a local legend, and I have been referred to as a legend by some camp higher ups! I always thought you had to be dead or something to be classified as a legend! So lets find the meaning to this word.

Legend- a traditional story sometimes popularly regarded as historical but unauthenticated.

This could be me, but I think people view me more hysterically than historically!

Legend–very well known

This could be me?

Legend- fable-story-tale-inscription-myth

This is definitely not me, unless I've been living in the twilight zone all my life? But for me this life has been all too real! So I will leave it up to you what you believe about the legend stuff! I agree with what Danielle Lahr had mentioned in church the other day. If we are truly followers of Jesus, then we should be trying to change the culture around us; not letting the culture around us, change us! So that is all I have ever tried to do these past 18 years and if that makes me a legend well so be it!

We checked into a motel in Gaffney and drove to Blacksburg to see Tracy's father's sister Annie Sue. Annie Sue is a person I would call a hoot! And I mean that in a good way! Annie Sue is 80 years old and she just couldn't quit telling Jordan how handsome he looked!

She told him he might just as well move down there with her! Make no mistake though Annie Sue is a deep Christian woman and about a devout as they come. She has a story of how Jesus healed her that would make any group of modern day doctors with the best of educations, walk away scratching their heads! We were going to drive over to the land that we came down to see and Annie Sue would have supper for us when we returned! The land was just a few miles out of town instead of an old dirt road that I was expecting the road was paved for most of the way out there! Annie Sue was to tell us latter that some relative of theirs knew somebody on the city council and it got paved! I suspect though that somebody ordered extra pavement for a job in town and the town of Blacksburg ended up paying for the road! I was telling Jordan several times on this trip as well as the rest of you younger people that may be reading this. It is not always what you know that is important, but who you know a lot of times will take you further! However it got done it was a surprise from what I had been expecting! There is an old house there made of logs but sided over. Annie Sue thought that her dad built it some 86 years ago. No one lived there since the 1960's. In what onetime was probably the front yard a tree had grown right through the center of a tire, the tree looked like it could be all of 40 years old! We set out to walk around the property. Jordan wanted to do some shooting so we were looking for a place to hang a target. We had to walk through some pretty thick thorns and pricker bushes to get down to one of the two natural springs that flow through the land. This all reminded me of my boyhood days exploring in the woods and going after cows! More than once I would come home all tore up. My mom would ask me what in the world did I get into! I would just laugh about it, but she never thought it very funny as she was the person who had to patch my clothes! When we reached the spring we took time out to pray. First we thanked God for this adventure we were on and also asked God for wisdom for Tracy what to do with these 26.25 acres of land now that it was in his care; after being in his family these many years! I don't know how the others felt at this moment, but for me to be there standing on a piece of American history asking God for wisdom what to do with it, was practically inexplicable and to me no small thing! Funny thing we said the prayer under a Sycamore tree and crossed the spring on a fallen Cedar tree just the opposite scenario of the Harbinger book by Jonathan Cain! We climbed up the opposite bank and were met by more briars! I was thinking about this time about the crown of thorns they put on Jesus head!

Matthew 27:29

They plaited a crown from branches of a thorn bush and set it on his head. They put a stick in his right hand for a scepter. Then they knelt before him in mocking reverence: "Bravo, King of the Jews!" they said. "Bravo!"

And I thought of how that must have felt! We decided we had to get out of those thorns, because our pants were getting wrecked! We finally did make it to our vehicle. At that point we each had a glass of wine and made a toast to new beginnings! After that I walked over to the old house and walked inside. Tracy thought the floor would be no good, but it was, thanks to the tin roof it had! Jordan and Tracy had me take a picture of them standing in the doorway. After wards we did do some shooting with Tracy's pistol. I thought it was loud and I'm more accurate with my lever action 22 or double barrel shot gun, but to each his own. After wards we drove to Annie Sue's for supper. She had her counters full of food and was taking a big roaster out of the oven I knew at that moment my diet was in jeopardy! While we were eating Annie Sue was telling stories of when she was a young person out there on that land. One was when they were kids how they used to swim in the dirty wash water after dirty overalls had been washed. I was amused with Jordan as I knew he wasn't getting the full meaning of Annie Sue's story! According to my mother years ago before modern day wash machines men would wear those overalls from a week to as long as a month before they would be washed. Imagine working around livestock and dirt for that length of time and I am almost certain the cleanser would be homemade lye soap. That was the kind of wash water Annie Sue would be playing in! Annie Sue was telling of another time when they had to go to the spring and get what she called "Their night water." During the daytime her mother had washed the clothes and hung them on bushes to dry as she didn't have a clothes line! It got dark on the kids on their way back from the spring and she said the clothes looked like "haints" up there on the bushes! Jordan asked what a haint was. A "spook" was Annie Sue's answer! So she meant the clothes looked like Haunts up there on the bushes! We all had a great laugh, and ate till we about burst! I think if I would have ate one more bite of anything I would have died! We left Annie Sue's and went back to the motel room for the evening, we were to pick up Annie Sue for breakfast, but it was more near noon before we got there. First we had to stop at a clothing store. Tracy and Jordan had to get a pair of pants to replace the ones that got tore up the day before! I know when I got out of the shower that morning, and was drying off my legs just killed! While we were looking for this clothing store I asked Tracy where it was. Tracy said his grandfather would have said "it was just down yon road a piece." He motioned his hand in the direction we were going. "How far is a piece," I asked? "About a mile" Tracy said. I was telling the guys that I had gained weight on this trip Tracy said " they call that you've fleshened up! "What do they call it when you need to lose weight?" "You need to fall off" Tracy answered. I said, "I need to go down yon a fer piece, and fall off!" Meaning when I get back home I need to lose this weight I gained on this trip! We were all laughing as we pulled into the parking lot at the clothing store. After that we had to stop off at the court house I had given Tracy some suggestions what he might do with his land. So it took us a little longer at the court house than we planned! After that we picked up Annie Sue and we went to Denny's restaurant. I forgot all we talked about over lunch, but afterward Annie Sue took us out past the home place to a little country church not far down the road. Annie Sue was telling us how the local moonshiners would take their whiskey and hide it at this church to avoid being caught by the revenue agents! I never asked Annie Sue how she knew all of this, perhaps I should have. We pulled up to an old cemetery near the church and She was showing Tracy where some of their people were buried. One of the stones showed 1791 for a birth date, and that's a long time ago! After we left the cemetery, we were on the way back to Annie Sue's house and she told us this story. Sometimes they would be too long in town and it would get dark on them coming home. Her daddy's ford T model didn't have any lights. So he would put Annie Sue up in front of the car with a flashlight and she would ride up there and light the way home! We prayed a blessing over Annie Sue before we left, and she has fast became one of my favorite people! I know face book has become very popular in our culture recently, but give me a few friends like Annie Sue and I could just sit around talking about the good old days until Jesus returns! Before we left Jordan told Annie Sue that she needed to come back home with him and cook for him and his friends at college. She told him she might just take him up on that someday! Those 19-20 year old guys are like filling a silo when it comes to eating, but I bet Annie Sue could do it easy enough! After we said good bye to Annie Sue we headed back to Virginia. Up in North Carolina the speed limit on this stretch of road was 60 miles an hour. Tracy always seems well aware of his surroundings; I noticed a high way patrol right in front of us. I held my tongue as the cop pulled into the left lane and Tracy drove right passed him! Immediately the cop pulled Tracy over for going 19 miles over the speed limit. I said a quick pray for Tracy but he got a ticket anyway! As I write this story, this happened not too far from fancy gap Virginia where they just had that 95 car crash on that stretch of road, because of fog! We got back to Tracy's parents that evening and went from people mowing lawns to people shoveling snow in just three hours. That night at supper time I had to get the correct version of this story Tracy likes to tell. It always cracks me up when I hear it, and I feel it's part of Americana and needs to be preserved! Gerrie's uncle George Lane was getting ready to go hunting one day as they needed the food, but George's wife also pointed out that they were about out of wood to cook and heat with. Sizing up the situation quickly George responded " Well honey I ain't taken the axe!" I guess George wasn't the nicest of people Tracy went on to tell his uncle George's wife name was Larkate but was spelled Laura Kate she had a son Tracy said sounded like it would be spelled Lewaserle the correct spelling is Lewis Earl I thought it sounded like lose Earl. So once again our mealtime was filled with lots of laughs! After supper Jordan hung a ceiling fan for his grandmother and I helped him a little, but was little help. We left

Gerrie and Howards right after breakfast to head for home I leave a far richer man Gerrie gave me a shirt, $20 for the trip home and a book called The Man that moved a Mountain, and a whole ton of stories!

Part 3 on the way home

Tracy decided that we would head up to see his sister Tonya these two have the same birthday but are 5 years apart that too I find unique! Tracy is the older of the 2. This would take us 250 miles straight north into Ohio. This was the first time I had seen West Virginia in the daylight I saw several places where they had coal piled up, and you could see the coal veins between the limestone rocks where they cut the road through the mountains. I thought of my friend Wayne back home he is always talking about finding some coal to burn. It looks like he could have all he wanted out in these parts, but I see more wood smoke coming out of chimneys than anything else! I sure did enjoy my time in the mountains, but I also enjoyed coming out of them into the rolling farm fields in Ohio. Near Lower Salem we pulled up to Tracy's sisters farm house. Where I was introduced to Tonya Davis, Tracy's sister and her daughters, Elisabeth, and Katharine. I found out during Lunch that Elisabeth has her own chickens that she raises and Katharine has 24 sheep that she mainly sells breeding stock! I don't know why I should be so impressed by all of that after all are not these two girls related to Annie Sue? I was also amazed to find out Katharine had spent some time out on a sheep ranch near Sisters Oregon. I was just in that town not 2 months ago when I was out visiting my sister Marie so I know exactly where it is! I'm sorry all this talk of chickens and sheep takes me back in time! I am well acquainted with both the critters! My dad had about 40 head of sheep at one time I bottle fed lots of lambs they are so cute I can still see there little tails wiggling as they feed! I liked shearing time too, and it was my job to haul hay to them every day in the winter we kept them at the end of the road and I would stack ten bales of hay on my big sled and hook our Shetland pony to it every day I would do this all winter long! And chickens let me tell you my mom had 500 of them at one time Bared Rocks and Road Island Reds! It was my job to collect the eggs once upon a time! Those chickens could get a little broody and they liked to peck me so I either went in there with a forked stick and poked there head against the wall so they couldn't get me while I collected their eggs, or sometimes I would ware winter gloves so if they did peck me it wouldn't hurt! I always think of that when somebody starts talking about chickens! Well anyway so much for memory lane! We had broccoli soup over bacon pieces and it was the first time I have ever had sheep's cheese. Normally I would not eat that kind of food but I figured I should try it and it was pretty good! Thanks all three of you for the great lunch that we had! After Ice cream we retreated to the living room to visit for a while. Tonya had a wood stove going alright real heat just like back home! Tonya mentioned that she had a family of Calvinists coming to spend the evening. I was telling Tonya that I thought we would be more fun than they would be! I said that for a joke not a slam to my Calvinist brothers and sisters in the Lord! Katharine and Tonya wanted Jordan to stay. Tracy made the comment that everybody wants Jordan to stay but they never say a thing about us George! Tonya said alright Jordan and George can stay! I have to say Tracy doesn't have too much effect on his sister I think she is used of his antics, and they have little effect on her. I have 2 sisters myself Tracy so I know how it works! After we left there we pretty much headed east. Amy Gould texted Tracy right when we got into her area so we were able to stop and visit with her and her friend Charlene. They were our cooks at camp for a few years, and sure enough Amy brought up the subject of Hornets right away! Jordan had concerns that we would never get home at this rate! Like we had anything real important to get home too! It was good to see Amy and Charlene again, and we did eventually get back to the Porters around 1 am. The next day we spent most of the day taking it easy. I could see that since we had left some purple crocuses had come up in the yard. Tracy was mentioning all the animals that were in the neighborhood. I was telling him that back home the pheasants walk right up to the house, and I joke with people I could have pheasant under glass anytime! Pheasant under glass to me is I lift up the window and shoot him from inside the house! Tracy thought that humorous and said I should have told that story to his mom because that is what she fixed for a meal the last time she was visiting! After while we went to take some bread to the church. Tracy was telling me that part of the city the church was in was what you call West Allis. I was telling Tracy that's where my favorite tractor was made at the Allis Chalmers co. In West Allis. My family has bought that brand since they switched from the horses and I own 2 of them myself. I had been trying to phone Ray and Denise Olson I had e-mailed them telling I would be down in the area and would stop in to see them if it would work for them when I left the Porters. I finally got a hold of Ray and made arrangements to go over the next afternoon. Right before I left Tracy asked if I would walk over his property with him. Right away I saw a pair of mourning doves on a tree limb a sure sign to me that God is up to something in these parts! Tracy was showing me some trees and bushes that needed to be removed. I was telling him that I could come back and do that for him and that Ray and Denise could use the fire wood. So it sounds like I will drive back down there the last weekend in April to do this. Tracy was showing me his roof it was close to needing shingling I was telling Tracy that Troy Meisner was in the roofing business and I'm sure he would be glad to come and do your roof. For some reason I seem to be the guy with the connections! Before I left Tracy, Cherie, Jordan, and Joseph prayed for me before I left, what a great time down at the Porters! After just 40 minutes of travel I arrived at Ray and Denise's pyramid off high way 33 near Beaver Dam Wisconsin. I found Ray out back collecting eggs when I drove in. I also had some old bread for their goats that was left over from Tracy's bread run at Panara. I was to call Rick Bengston when we figured out what we were going to do that evening. Denise would not be there that evening so Ray, Rick, and I went to The Sports bar/grill in Beaver Dam. Rick left around 10:30 pm and I went to bed. I have come to know Rick from being part of camps I'd say about 4-5 years now. Half way through the night the 2 cats jumped on the bed and scared me! Ray had some coffee ready when I got up. We were talking when Denise got home. I have come to know Ray and Denise through Illinois youth camp, servants passage, snow blast, the Dells, and Ky staying here the growing season of 2005. All of 9 years now. After I left Ray and Denise I headed for Spring Valley Minnesota. I was going to spend the evening at Troy Meisner's house, and go to Rochester Grace Communion Church the next morning. Troy was in the process of making Maple syrup when I arrived. Troy is one of the three pastors at Rochester Church. It seems like I have known Troy forever he is one of my longest friends from this fellowship. I met Troy not long after I came into the WWCG back in June 17 1995. And I have known his sons Ian and Hunter for as long as they have been alive! I view Troy as one of the most level headed people I know that seems to be a rare trait these days! We were going to have steaks but they were so thick I told Troy we could stack them and cook them like a roast. Troy asked how I cook roast. I told him I just put it in a roaster frozen put pepper on it and a onion and bake at 350 for 3 hours. Troy ask me how I knew for sure it was done. I told Troy If smoke fly's out of the oven you know for sure it is done. I know Troy tolerates my humor, because he laughs and says George, George, George. After a great meal a board game and homemade Ice cream it was time for bed. We all had to get up early as the youth had to make the breakfast and start serving at 8 am. When I walked into church there were 2 young friends that I hadn't seen in a while Josh Craig and Sam Maki both of the guys were former campers from Northern light and Snow Blast. And once upon a time I was their councilor. Sam Maki was down visiting his dad David who lives at my house. One time Sam bought his dad to the pumpkin thing and he worked for me after that. David has been here on and off for 3 years now, and I've probably known Sam for 6. Sam lives in Cook Minnesota a town straight north from my place about 5.45 hours away. I just told Sam that it was good to see him and that I hoped he enjoyed my house while he was there! Josh Craig was kind of a rough customer when he was at camp! I had to kick him out of our dorm the last evening because he let's just say he was acting up! I did this even if he was the camp director's nephew; which just happened to be the guy speaking today Todd Fox. As I recall the Holy Spirit was impressing upon me to end the camp in a positive way as far as Josh was concerned so I kept looking for an opportunity. Often I have seen

God work things out the last possible second, that's how you know it is God as it was nothing you have done! Josh came up to me that last day after camp was pretty much done and wanted to shake my hand. I think I told him I wouldn't shake his hand,

But I would give him a hug! Josh was sobbing when he told me that he was sorry for what he had done. I told him he was forgiven and that he should have a great rest of the summer. I hope Josh reads this someday, as I am still in the mindset that it takes a big man to admit that he was wrong! So when Todd Fox asked his audience what gets them excited after several comments Josh raised his hand and said "Seeing George here." God showed me that I had made an impact on Joshes life.

> Matthew 11:16-19
>
> But to what shall I liken this generation? It is like children sitting in the marketplaces and calling to their companions, 17 and saying: 'We played the flute for you, And you did not dance; We mourned to you, And you did not lament.' 18 For John came neither eating nor drinking, and they say, 'He has a demon.' 19 The Son of Man came eating and drinking, and they say, 'Look, a glutton and a winebibber, a friend of tax collectors and sinners!' But wisdom is justified by her children

Josh isn't the first person I had to get tough on, but it just goes to show a little old fashioned tough love isn't that bad neither! After services I went over to Josh and gave him a hug! After chatting with Josh a while, and a few others it was time for me to come home. I hadn't been there in 9 days, when I left everything was covered in snow, but the further I drove east the snow was less and less. When

I got home there was only a patch of snow here and there, and the Lake was showing signs of opening up. The first thing I did when I got home was to change into my favorite pair of bib overalls! Then I walked outside and opened the double doors on my machine shed it is my declaration that springtime has come! Then I went right to work I came back into the house and wrote this story. I have learned from experience that when God gives me one of these story's to write it is best if I take the time and do it. Or he will make sure that I have all the time I need to do it. Like I mentioned earlier a little bit of tough love isn't the worst thing in the world for a person!

This past winter I have been from Oregon to South Carolina, and even met people from other countries. Through all my travels and whomever I have met, alongside of me my very best friend has been. He is Jesus the Christ, and he has this to say to you all.

John 15:12-17

This is my command: Love one another the way I loved you. 13 This is the very best way to love. Put your life on the line for your friends. 14 You are my friends when you do the things I command you. 15 I'm no longer calling you servants because servants don't understand what their master is thinking and planning. No, I've named you friends because I've let you in on everything I've heard from the Father. 16 "You didn't choose me, remember; I chose you, and put you in the world to bear fruit, fruit that won't spoil. As fruit bearers, whatever you ask the Father in relation to me, he gives you. 17 "But remember the root command: Love one another.

And I am sure we are all in agreement, all the friends that I have written about. That He Is Risen He Is Risen Indeed!

Matthew 28:1-8

1 After the Sabbath, as the first light of the new week dawned, Mary Magdalene and the other Mary came to keep vigil at the tomb. 2 Suddenly the earth reeled and rocked under their feet as God's angel came down from heaven, came right up to where they were standing. He rolled back the stone and then sat on it. 3 Shafts of lightning blazed from him. His garments shimmered snow-white. 4 The guards at the tomb were scared to death. They were so frightened, they couldn't move. 5 The angel spoke to the women: "There is nothing to fear here. I know you're looking for Jesus, the One they nailed to the cross. 6 He is not here. He was raised, just as he said. Come and look at the place where he was placed. 7 "Now, get on your way quickly and tell his disciples, 'He is risen from the dead. He is going on ahead of you to Galilee. You will see him there.' That's the message." 8 The women, deep in wonder and full of joy, lost no time in leaving the tomb. They ran to tell the disciples.

Have a great resurrection day my friends spring is here!
in Christ,
George Denn

# Hey by George! May 22-25 2013

# THE BINDER AND THE CROSS!

Zephaniah 3:14-17

So sing, Daughter Zion! Raise the rafters, Israel! Daughter Jerusalem, be happy! celebrate! 15 God has reversed his judgments against you and sent your enemies off chasing their tails. From now on, God is Israel's king, in charge at the center. There's nothing to fear from evil ever again! God Is Present Among You 16 Jerusalem will be told: "Don't be afraid. Dear Zion, don't despair. 17 Your God is present among you, a strong Warrior there to save you. Happy to have you back, he'll calm you with his love and delight you with his songs.

One day about a month ago, I was looking on the Internet. I thought perhaps I could find a better grain binder than I had! My search lead me to companies that made brand new self-propelled ones out of India. The only problem they could not be brought into the U.S.A. because they did not meet our pollution standards! Also they had a price of $13,500 a sum far too much for me to come up with for a machine I only use on 2 acres! Running my old horse drawn McCormick Deering seemed to be in my future for one more year. Which usually turns into nothing less than a hair raising experience, with this rickety relic from the past! For some reason I typed in John Deere Grain binder into my search engine. Almost immediately I found one on Craig's list for $1000 near West Bend Wisconsin. I found this sort of peculiar as I would be in that area for the next 4 days only 30 miles south of there cutting trees and brush for a friend Tracy Porter in Peewaukee Wisconsin.

Originally I had decided to go down to Tracy's a week later than I did, but I thought as long as it was too wet for field work, I should do it earlier than planned. Perhaps the fields would be dry that last weekend in April the time I would be gone? I would take a look at the binder before I went to Tracy's. On my way I was going through the Wisconson Dell's I pulled off on exit 89 for gas, but after filling up my pickup with gas I found out the starter had went out, so I was stranded! Trying not to get too excited I pulled out the towing service card I had in my billfold and called the number. After some questions from a machine a real live human actually came on the line. It took longer to make the arrangements to be towed than to get towed. A place called Platt's towing came and got me. Platt's Garage is located right in Lake Delton, they had a new starter in my truck in just a few minutes, and I was on my way. I was a little mad that I had to spend $225 on a repair because this was just a weekend to help out some friends it had nothing to do with money. No good deed goes unpunished is a saying I thought of, but almost as fast the Lord said just wait the weekend isn't over yet! I was able to look at the binder and gave Chad it's owner $500 down with the balance to be paid the day I picked it up, this was fine with Chad. This grain binder was new in 1950, way newer than the one I had from 1925, and the few acres I have to cut with it should last as long as I need it! Also it was pto driven, and not ground driven so it should run way smother. Afterwards I drove down to Tracy's, and only got lost once. It was getting dark and was very foggy so I was glad when I pulled into Porter's drive! The next few days were spent sawing wood, chipping brush, and hauling the firewood up to Ray and Denise Olson's. Their church will use it for a fire at various times during the year. On Saturday April 20 we celebrated my 51 birthday. Besides Tracy and Cherie, Chris and Sarah Phelps, and Rick Bengston was there. What a great time we had I still wonder most days where all those years went to? Some days I feel like one of those old cow poke cartoon characters my favorite one is this cow boy is sitting in the bank talking to his banker he tells his banker " why don't you give me one of those student loans till I can figure out what it is i'm a doin!" Sometimes I tell young people that I'm still trying to figure out what I want to do when I grow up! They usually think this is funny, truthfully though I'm doing what I always wanted to do whatever that is, a farmer I guess! On Monday before I left Tracy told me that God had impressed upon him to give me $200 towards my starter trouble and earlier had filled me with gas so I figured that more than made up for my repair! Tracy also gave me a book called Surprised by the voice of God, how God speaks today through prophesies, dreams, and visions by Jack Deere. I thought it was interesting how on my way down I bought a John Deere grain binder and on my way home I was given a book written by Jack Deere. It made me re member my mom's dad his name was John, but every one called him Jack! I stopped by Ray and Denise's to take back their chipper I had borrowed, and to have lunch with them, after lunch I headed for home. I saw 2 guy's out in the field on hwy 33 on the way home, an Amish farmer had planted some oat's, and another man had torn up an alfalfa stand that had died during the winter. I was to find out a week later that all of my hay ground had died out too! When I got to Minnesota it was raining most of the way until I got to almost Owatonna when the rain turned to snow! The traffic slowed down to 30 miles an hour. I had to follow this van that was driving so slow for more than 30 miles. Those who tried to pass ended up in the ditch so I resisted the urge to pass! We ended up with 6 inches of snow so I had plenty of time to read the book Tracy had given me to read! I called my friend Howard Guse to see if he would haul the binder someday for me, he said he would, but it would be a few weeks. The next weekend I found out my hay had all died! So much for the $66,000 it all would have sold for this year, as well as the $5000 I had to invest in re seeding. Time to start looking too God once again for my provision, but isn't that the way it is supposed to be anyway? I got my neighbor David Gibson to work the ground for me so I could plant. David tried to get me to wait a few days more so the ground would be dryer, but I thought it was fit enough, besides they were predicting rain for the next week. After a couple of days even David himself said it was a good thing we had gotten it in! The snow that we had seemed to pack the ground so it would not dry very fast! One early afternoon while we were waiting for the soil to dry a man drove in my yard with a big motorcycle. He introduced himself as Greg Thomas. Greg told me that he had read my books, and he just had to meet me! He was going on and on about how much my stories had touched his life, he even read my first book to his friend David Crooner one night over the telephone! I was sort of amused by all of this that something I had written had touched someone so deeply! I had been down earlier in the day over the weather. I was telling Greg that I couldn't write anything that day if my life depended on it I needed to be inspired by the Holy Spirit to do so! Greg stuck around for 5 hours! He was telling me his story how he had asked Jesus into his heart and life and how Jesus had healed him of stage 4 cancer! He was telling of this little white country church he was fixing up that hadn't been used in more than 70 years! He showed me the news clip from the channel 11 news had done on him and his project of love! He was telling me how the folks who made the movie Memorial Day had used the little church as well as finding himself becoming one of the actors! Greg read some of the stories he had wrote and mentioned that he would like to publish them, but didn't know how to go about that, so I was able to show him how I went about it, and how to connect with the publisher. I knew Greg's stopping like he did was out of the ordinary and God was up to something just what I couldn't see at the moment! Greg was mentioning before he left about a cross planting at the church someday in the near future. I told Greg I would be interested in coming to that and he should let me know when it was to be. Greg mentioned that he was going to write a story about meeting me so I have included that here!

Road Trip May 7, 2013

Last week it was my turn to clean Life 21, the church that I attend in Northfield MN. As I got out all the cleaning supplies from the janitor closet, I walked past the book and DVD rack we have in the hallway. These are available to anyone who would like to sign them out to read or view. I glanced at the rack as I was cleaning and about four rows down; I spotted a book called "Hey by George." The title grabbed my attention as well as, the old photograph on the book cover. I picked up the book, and there was a second book behind the first with the same title, so I grabbed that one too. I took both of the books home and started reading the first one as I lay in bed that evening. It didn't register in my brain at the time; but, as I began reading the first book I started thinking I had seen that saying somewhere before? Finally, it came to my mind that I had seen a 4x8 sheet of plywood nailed halfway up a telephone pole, with bright florescent orange paint; depicting the words; "Hey by George." This I had seen nearly a year ago, while driving out in the country on my way to do some shopping in Mankato. After delving into the book a little father; it became apparent that the book I was reading was written by the man who made the sign I had seen a year previous! His stories that he has written, are about his life on a farm; and God's hand in all that he encounters. They are to say the least, humorous, witty, fun to read, ponder, and each one, gives glory to God! If you get a chance, look them up on the web. "Hey By George" author; George Denn. Through reading his books; I found inspiration, and realized that this man only lived 35 miles from me! I just knew that this was someone that I had to meet; and as I was at the coffee shop in New Prague the following morning, I prayed about being able to meet with him. I said, Lord if you want me to meet with this man, give me a sign. As I was walking out the front door of the coffee shop, a pickup truck with a huge load of hay passed by right by in front of me! I said, done deal! Thank you Lord! It was a beautiful day out and I went home to get out my motorcycle. I grabbed everything that I wanted to share with George; loaded it on my bike, and I was off. I was agonizing over the fact that I was coming unannounced; and prayed that I wouldn't disturb him if he was busy working. I pulled up his long drive way and shut off my bike in front of the farm house. As I was pulling off my helmet, he stepped out the front door and greeted me with a hello. He didn't know me from Adam; So, I started with that very fact; I told him of my cleaning the church, and discovering his books and I knew we just had to meet. We sat down at his picnic table in the front lawn and five hours later we wrapped up our conversation's. I met his hired hand Dave, who also joined us and was a pleasure to meet. We ended our conversation with George leading us in prayer and then I also, prayed and thanked God for this awesome encounter with George and Dave. George told me that, he had been feeling down that day, but, God had picked him back up after we had met. I am totally convinced that this was not a chance meeting; but by God's design. I just met two new friends; that are members of the kingdom of God, and I know we are destined to meet again soon. Road trips to me are always an adventure, waiting for a place to happen. God sent me on this one to encourage a brother in Christ who was feeling down. As a result; we were all lifted up! When God does something; he does it all the way! This was a road trip I will never forget!!! As I am writing this I paused and said a short prayer that God would speak to me through his word. I opened my bible to Isaiah 50: 4 it says: The Lord God has given me his words of wisdom. He does this so I will know what I should say to all these tired ones. Morning by morning he awakens me. He opens my understanding to his will. George, Dave, you spoke to me, as much as I spoke to you! Blessings in Christ, Greg

The next day I was able to get my wheat seeded with my neighbor David's help again. Once again he thought I should wait! I finished that day in the rain I know God was helping me, because if I would have had to go across that field once more I never would have made it the grain drill was getting clogged with mud just as I was finishing up! I was soaking wet but as the song goes I'm no stranger to the rain! It would be another week before I could finish up planting my oats! The next week was spent cutting firewood and I finished up with oats planting on May 14 about a month later than normal! In there somewhere Howard called we planned to go to West Bend the next day to pick up the grain binder, but we had to call it off, because Howard's truck was having transmission problems, and had to send it to a shop to be fixed before we could make the trip! My friend Steve Morabu from Kenya Africa has been helping me for a few days. I showed him how to drive the skid loader, so he had me take like a video on his phone. He calls it Minnesota axe man! I don't think his friends believed him so he needed some proof as to what he was doing! Howard called me on May 20 he said we could go get the binder the next day as his pickup transmission was fixed! I called Chad and told him we would be down the next day sometime in the afternoon as it was a six hour drive from here. I drove over to Howard's the next morning and we left at 7:30 we noticed as we drove that there was practically no field work done between Rochester MN, and the Wisconsin Dells. I was telling Howard that we needed to be thankful for what we had planted. Near West Bend Howard's transmission started acting funny it clunked a couple of times and you could feel it in the cab when it did that! I was telling Howard that I hoped we could at least make it to where the binder was! We did and had it loaded in about half an hour it only weighed a ton so it wasn't much heavier on the truck than the trailer was already. We made it back to exit 92 at the Dells as Howard was making the exit it totally quit pulling in drive! We were able to get to a gas station to park, everything there was under construction, and one lane only so we would have caused quite a commotion if the transmission had totally went out! Howard checked the oil in the transmission it didn't look all that low but he put a quart in, and said " let's see if it works now" it didn't! We had to go back up on hwy 90 and exit on exit 89 to get to a station that had diesel fuel. We ended up at the same station where my starter had gone out a month earlier! I was telling Howard that this Wisconsin Dells seems like the Bermuda triangle for vehicles! After Howard filled with fuel he called the place that had fixed his truck a week earlier after the call we weighed our options. We could call Platt's towing here in town they could tow it, and fix it or we could drive 40 miles an hour all the way home 300 miles! Howard choose to drive home. I told Howard what we needed was for the Holy Spirit to enter his transmission, so I said a prayer for that as we were leaving the station! For a while we were only able to go 40 miles an hour on interstate 90 which wasn't the worst because traffic could get around us, but then we came to a section of road that was one lane for about 20 miles. We had 4 semi's and 70 cars backed up behind us! Howard and I were laughing, because we knew that the many vehicles that were behind us were probably not viewing us in a positive way, but we were helpless to do anything about the situation at this point! Howard said he may have an idea that would help us go faster. He was messing with his cruise control button the one that increases the speed by a mile an hour. We were gaining speed first 45 miles an hour than 50 Howard mentioned that he didn't know how much more he could do that without having his transmission fail again. He got it up to 60 than 65 by the time we got to Minnesota we were going 75! I was telling Howard that we were experiencing a miracle, as I never heard of a transmission getting better and better, they always get worse and worse! Howard was trying to surmise what might be taking place. I told Howard that sometimes we try to explain things when all we really have to do is realize that God is at work, we are experiencing a miracle, and leave it at that! We made it home fine, just 2 hours later than we should have. The cross planting was to be held at Greg's church the next morning all I knew at the moment that was that I just wanted to get home and get to sleep! We were to meet at Greg's church at 10 am it was almost an hour drive so we had to leave around 9. I was awakened at 6 am to rain I thought that moment about my dad's old saying rain before 7 clear by 11, but that day it would not be so! I got up took a bath and got ready for the day wondering with anticipation what this day would bring forth! I knew I had a story to write I even had a title to it, but I had to wait until the day played out so I could start to write. David Maki rode with me and when we arrived at St John's Catholic church I went by and turned right onto another gravel country road so as not to be a hindrance to the activity that was about to take place. Wayne Schwartz had called and said he wouldn't be working that day so he would meet us there later. Two guys were there one with a John Deere tractor and loader, one with a lull loader. I walked across the church lawn in the rain and introduced myself. First to Bob Krocak a neighbor of the church. Bob mentioned that we had met before at Smiths mill Implement some years ago although I can just vaguely remember. Bob is a dairy farmer from the area and he mentioned that his great grandfather helped build this little country church. The other Guy was Don Rynda he was the owner of the John Deere tractor I recognized Don from the channel 11 news clip that Greg had shown me a few weeks earlier! Don also is an area farmer retired I think, but he still helps his son. I guess if you are a true farmer you never really retire it gets in your blood and is sometimes more important than breathing to you! Don is also head of the cemetery association that cemetery is located near the church. After a few minutes person after person showed up. There was Pastors Bill and Carol Mantal from the Christian cyber ministries. They are the ones in charge of planting these huge crosses all over the world this was to be cross #52! One of his board members in this ministry Kirk Glassen was there to assist in the assembly of the 30'x20'x8"x 8" cross. Tom Mariska owns the farm west of the church it was his great grandmother that donated the land that the church and cemetery sits on Tom is 87 and never remembers a time that the church had been in use a sign in front of the church says founded in 1856! Dar Kline was a interesting person to meet she goes to Greg's church in North field Mn. she seemed like she liked giving everyone hugs and was holding an umbrella for most of the day! She seemed amused when I told her I used to cheat in typing class back in high school I passed with a D. I am sure that I was amusing God back then for I figured who needs this stuff any way I was going to be a farmer and what would a farmer have use for typing any way! Now I wish that I would have applied myself a little more than I had! I was also telling Dar that I had a connection to North field through the outlaw Jesse James. My Great, Great Grandfather Jacob Peter Denn and his sons cleared more than 600 acres of this wooded Minnesota territory some miles south of Mankato. This was all done with axes, saws, horses, stump pullers, and latter dynamite! One day Jacob was hauling logs out of the woods with a Percheron stallion that he had imported from France. Frank and Jesse stuck a gun barrel in Jacobs gut and took his horse, probably it was the one that took them back to Missouri. This is all documented in some papers my dad has! David Cooner a friend of Greg's was also there. David is the guy Greg read one of my books to over the telephone one evening in its entirety! I gave David a set of those books so he can read them for himself. Wayne Schwartz showed up shortly after I got there I invited Wayne he is Catholic I figured he would greatly appreciate the history of this place. Wayne is one of my landlords, my full time mechanic, and good friend. Wayne wanted me to make sure everyone knows that he is on my staff! Although I am not quite sure what he thinks that will do for him, it amused me any way! I saw David Maki getting involved with assembling the cross beams I was glad David came with I think the day did something for him. Henry Schindel from New Prague MN was there. Greg said Henry and his wife would stop by the church from time to time while he was working out there and Greg would pray for them Henrys wife has past away since. Phil and Karen Saari were present Karen is Greg's sister. The man responsible for all us being there as well as supplying cookies and coffee Greg Thomas! Oops almost forgot Marty Krocak, Bobs son was their later on to assist Bob as they made the cross secure for the cement to harden in the hole. A prayer was said inside the little church before we started the process and after a plaque was attached to the cross after it was secure in the ground this whole process took about 5 hours and it rained every moment we were there! The whole day just seemed inexplicable to me and I felt very privileged to be amongst those who were there, most who I had met for the first time! A thought came into my head as I stood in the green country church yard that rainy day near Montgomery Minnesota, some 40 miles from where I live. In his book the Harbinger, Jonathan Cain writes how "the ancient is bound to the modern!" I felt it was no small thing that I had been a part of that day, and what had drawn me there that rainy mid-May day. It was quite possibly one of the most important seeds that were planted in the area this spring! Here is the web site with pictures what

went on that day you can also see the channel 11 news story Greg showed me on the bottom of the page. Also a story Greg himself wrote about the day!
http://www.christiancyberministries.org/ccmEvents/menu_343.htm

Be Wide Awake! May 23, 2013

Yesterday was to say the least, an overwhelming experience for me. This was to be the day that a huge cross was to be planted out at the church that I have been restoring. This was being done by Christian Cyber Ministries out of Cambridge Minn. to give glory to God, for what he has brought forth out of a willing heart to serve him. I had no idea the emotions this would generate in me as the time grew closer to the day of the planting. The night before the planting, I was up past midnight; baking cookies for everyone that might show up for this event. I eventually went to bed and fell fast asleep; but awoke shortly after 3:00a.m. And knowing that slumber was not going to return, I got back up. They had been forecasting rain since the beginning of the week; right through Wednesday and I had been praying for a dry day for this historic event. It was raining when I awoke; and it never let up, as morning fast approached. I knelt on the floor in front of my recliner and prayed again for the rain to let up, and then I started praying for the day to unfold. A wave of emotions came over me, so much so, that I couldn't put them in words. I began praying in tongues and the Holy Spirit gave way to utterance, as wave after wave of emotions came to the surface. This was a day, I would not soon forget! A half a box of Kleenex later, I was off to the church to unlock the doors and get things set up. The first miracle of the day was, Bob Krocak was already there with the

Lull to lift the cross in place, when the time arrived. If you know Bob, being punctual is not one of his fortes, so this was definitely a miracle! Don Rynda was also there with the tractor, drag blade, and front end loader. Pastor Bill and Pastor Carol Mantel soon showed up, as well as Kirk Gassen; Pastor Bill's helper; in assembling the cross. Soon more people showed up; George Denn, Wayne Schwartz, David Maki, Dar Kline, Dave Cooner, Tom Mariska, Karen and Phil Saari, Marty Kroack, Henry Shindel. Everyone present played an important role in this cross being planted in the ground. Everyone was soaked to the bone, by the time this cross was in the ground; as the rain never let up! My prayer was not answered for dry weather for this event; later that day God told me why. I found out that Don, Bob, George, Wayne, David, Bill, and Marty would not have been there if the weather was dry, as they would of all been out in the field; planting their crops! Thank God For Un-Answered Prayer! God in his infinite wisdom provided everything we needed to see this thing through; from heavy equipment, to tools, generator, refreshments, shelter, man power, and even rain! We huddled in the church and formed a circle as we held hands, as Pastor Bill led us in prayer; Pastor Carol was next; and then I prayed last; Giving God glory for this day and the blessings he is bringing forth. We went outside and in the rain Pastor Bill applied the plaque to the front of the cross that proclaimed Gods Glory and another prayer of blessing was given. I am still tearing up as I write this, but as I tap out these letters on my computer, let me share what God gave me from 2nd Chronicles 6: 40,41 as I opened my bible this morning: Yes, O my God, be wide awake! Listen to all the prayers made to you in this place. And now, O Lord God, arise! Enter this resting place of yours. This is where the Ark of your strength has been put. Let your priests, O Lord God, be clothed with salvation. Let your people have joy in the kind deeds you do. My prayer for all of us today that are reading this is; may we "all" be "Wide Awake" to receive Christ as our Lord and personal savior; Greg Thomas

Just before I left the church that day Howard called and wondered when he could drop off my binder. I told Howard I was just finishing up what I was doing, so he said he would bring it over late afternoon early evening. After we unloaded the machine and put it in the shed I told Howard to come in the house so I could pay him for the hauling of the binder. Howard mentioned that the pickup was shifting funny again, hmm interesting! I just got off the phone with Howard I had to see what he had found out with his transmission as he took it back in to be looked at, and a few days had gone by. Evidently there was some sort of censer/switch on the side of the transmission that hooks up to the computer of the vehicle that helps with the automatic gear shifting. Howard said that after removing this censer/switch the mechanic told Howard that water just ran out of it into his hand! I find that interesting, and as I told Howard running water is a symbol of the Holy Spirit, and if you recall I asked the Holy Spirit to enter Howard's Transmission that day it was acting up for only he truly knew what our problem was! And this part sits alongside the transmission I don't know about all of you but I find that very interesting like an answer to a prayer! So how do you tie a grain binder and the cross together other than the fact that I just did, here is something interesting.

Leviticus 23:9-14

God spoke to Moses: 10 "Tell the People of Israel, When you arrive at the land that I am giving you and reap its harvest, bring to the priest a sheaf of the first grain that you harvest. 11 He will wave the sheaf before God for acceptance on your behalf; on the morning after Sabbath, the priest will wave it. 12 On the same day that you wave the sheaf, offer a year-old male lamb without defect for a Whole-Burnt-Offering to God 13 and with it the Grain-Offering of four quarts of fine flour mixed with oil–a Fire-Gift to God, a pleasing fragrance–and also a Drink-Offering of a quart of wine. 14 Don't eat any bread or roasted or fresh grain until you have presented this offering to your God. This is a perpetual decree for all your generations to come, wherever you live

It talks of the wave sheaf offering something that pointed to Jesus the Lamb of God. It was a bundle of barley the first sheaf cut out of a field in the season they didn't us twine back then to tie the sheaves like they did when machines were created they used a small hand full of the straw with the grain still attached to tie around the upright stalks of grain to make a sheaf. about 140 years ago some body invented a machine that tied a piece of twine around the cut stalks of grain eliminating the slower process done for centuries previous. Today Just a few of these machines still exist mostly used by Amish or a guy like me who has something unique going on. I use this machine for a couple of acres of wheat every year long before the crop is ripe. I make these sheaves of wheat to sell with my pumpkins and squash every year. This is something I have dedicated to God in my life, and has turned into what has been called " A Ministry of

Joy!" The cross most folks know it is a Christian symbol, because they crucified Jesus the Lamb of God on one!

John 19:17-22

Carrying his cross, Jesus went out to the place called Skull Hill (the name in Hebrew is Golgotha), 18 where they crucified him, and with him two others, one on each side, Jesus in the middle. 19 Pilate wrote a sign and had it placed on the cross. It read: Jesus the Nazarene the king of the Jews. 20 Many of the Jews read the sign because the place where Jesus was crucified was right next to the city. It was written in Hebrew, Latin, and Greek. 21 The Jewish high priests objected. "Don't write," they said to Pilate, "'The King of the Jews.' Make it, 'This man said, "I am the King of the Jews."'" 22 Pilate said, "What I've written, I've written."

That same Lamb of God binds us together with a cord that can't be broken!

Revelation 7:9-17

I looked again. I saw a huge crowd, too huge to count. Everyone was there—all nations and tribes, all races and languages. And they were standing, dressed in white robes and waving palm branches, standing before the Throne and the Lamb 10 and heartily singing: Salvation to our God on his Throne! Salvation to the Lamb! 11 All who were standing around the Throne–Angels, Elders, Animals–fell on their faces before the Throne and worshiped God, 12 singing: Oh, Yes! The blessing and glory and wisdom and thanksgiving, The honor and power and strength, To our God forever and ever and ever! Oh, Yes! 13 Just then one of the Elders addressed me: "Who are these dressed in white robes, and where did they come from?" 14 Taken aback, I said, "O Sir, I have no idea–but you must know." 15 That's why they're standing before God's Throne. They serve him day and night in his Temple. The One on the Throne will pitch his tent there for them: 16 no more hunger, no more thirst, no more scorching heat. 17 The Lamb on the Throne will shepherd them, will lead them to spring waters of Life. And God will wipe every last tear from their eyes."

In closing I am reminded of an old hymn that had been sung in our churches across this land long before I even existed, but its words have just as much meaning for us today as the people who lived before our times. The same Holy Spirit that inspired this hymn inspires us today. He inspired me to write this story you just read!

Bringing in the Sheaves.

Sowing in the morning sowing seeds of kindness sowing in the noontide and the dewy eve waiting for our harvest and the time of reaping we shall come rejoicing bringing in the sheaves refrain-twice Bringing in the sheaves bringing in the sheaves we will come rejoicing bringing in the sheaves

Sowing in the sunshine sowing in the shadows fearing neither clouds nor winters chilling breeze by and by the harvest and the labor ended we shall come rejoicing bringing in the sheaves

Refrain-twice

Going forth and weeping sowing for the master through the loss sustained our spirit often grieves when our weeping's over he will bid us welcome we shall come rejoicing bringing in the sheaves refrain-twice

So I guess the ancient really is bound to the modern after all!

Gods' peace and blessings to you all!

In Christ George Denn

**Hey by George! November 5, 2013**

# MEMORIES, MINISTRY, MONEY ORDERS, AND MIRACLES!

Ecclesiastes 3:9-15

9 But in the end, does it really make a difference what anyone does? 10 I've had a good look at what God has given us to do–busywork, mostly. 11 True, God made everything beautiful in itself and in its time–but he's left us in the dark, so we can never know what God is up to, whether he's coming or going. 12 I've decided that there's nothing better to do than go ahead and have a good time and get the most we can out of life. 13 That's it–eat, drink, and make the most of your job. It's God's gift. 14 I've also concluded that whatever God does, that's the way it's going to be, always. No addition, no subtraction. God's done it and that's it. That's so we'll quit asking questions and simply worship in holy fear. 15 Whatever was, is. Whatever will be, is. That's how it always is with God.

B oy where has the year gone here it is November already and I have been thinking of writing this story since haying time back in August! There is this hayfield that is slightly west, and across the road from where I live for 46 years this field has been part of my life and the goings on down there has had an important part of shaping my life. As I work harvesting hay in this field my mind very easily wanders back in time! The year is 1967 and this 5 year old boy is riding with dad as he cuts hay in the big slough as we called it. I noticed a sight in the hay field across the road. I told my dad I wanted to get off and run around some, he told me that was fine, but don't go across the road! What I really wanted to do was cross the road and look closely at what I saw there! So I waited for dad to get out of sight and my journey into another world began, I crossed the road! I sat in the tall grass in the road ditch and watched our neighbor Martin cutting his hay. He wasn't using a tractor like my dad, but had 2 horses pulling his hay mower try as I might at this young age I couldn't understand why this difference. I was fascinated by this scene. In my mind I can still see those two horses the harness creaking, the trace chains jingling on the eveners, and a friendly hello from the grampaish looking man in bib overalls riding on the iron seat of the hay mower as they passed me by! This scene gets interrupted by my dad as he laughingly asked me why I crossed the road. So for those of you out there wondering why I never seem to listen to anybody as you can see this all started at a very young age! Another memory flashes through my mind its 1976 and this 14 year old in well patched bib overalls goes to help neighbor Martin put up his hay this would take a week in the heat of the August sun. I drove the B John Deere on the hay loader as Martin leveled the load until it looked like a giant loaf of bread. Then we would take the load of hay up underneath the giant barn door Martin hooked the slings of hay to the block and tackle system I drove the B Farmall in reverse as I watched the slings of loose hay go straight up 30 feet when the carrier hit the trip in a 90 degree angle the sling of hay zoomed through the door and into the big red barn. I can still hear the clickety clack of that Minnesota hay loader and the sight of loose hay being pulled into the barn! After a week of this work I was paid the handsome sum of $1. This still amuses me to this day I never cared about the money I was just glad to be able to help a friend who was nearing his 80's by this time. Martin and his wife Hattie died with more than a million dollars in their possession so he probably could have spared a few dollars more! I was telling that story to someone once and he told me that I was one of the lucky ones not many people got a dollar out of that guy! A few years later my journey in life found me 3 miles away on a corn shelling crew on the George and Ester Olson farm. They were very good friends of Martin and Hattie. Ester raised white leghorn chickens she had about 500 of them one was being picked on by the others. So to save its life she gave it to Martin and Hattie who butchered the chicken and ate it! This dismayed the Olson's so much that a friendship of 50 years came to an end, over a leghorn chicken that if memory serves me correctly hasn't much meat on them anyway! Although these Old people made it almost impossible for young people like myself to succeed in life I still look back with fondness at them. I never had to live through the Great Depression it must have did something to them, as I grew older I made up my mind I didn't want to be like those people, and as I came to see God at work in my life I wanted to have deep friendships and give in a way that it would make a difference.

Matthew 7:7-12

7 "Don't bargain with God. Be direct. Ask for what you need. 8 This isn't a cat-and-mouse, hide-and-seek game we're in. 9 If your child asks for bread, do you trick him with sawdust? 10 If he asks for fish, do you scare him with a live snake on his plate? 11 As bad as you are, you wouldn't think of such a thing. You're at least decent to your own children. So don't you think the God who conceived you in love will be even better? 12 "Here is a simple, rule-of-thumb guide for behavior: Ask yourself what you want people to do for you, then grab the initiative and do it for them. Add up God's Law and Prophets and this is what you get.

Last April I was down in Wisconsin helping my friend Tracy Porter Clean up his grove of trees. Tracy had given me this book listening to the voice of God. In the course of conversation Tracy mentioned that a mutual friend Britta Lahr had asked his church for some financial help to do some ministry for inner city youth out in Colorado. I asked Britta to share her part of this story you are about to read. I will include Britta's side of this story at the end of what I write. Britta is a young woman that I meet several years back at S.E.P. camp and like any other friend I have I have come to enjoy Britta's friendship immensely! Britta never asked me if I would donate this year like she had last year. I felt I should ask her if she still needed some funds for her ministry. I was asking God how much to send her but I never got a clear answer like I did the year previous so I asked Britta how much she needed to reach her goal she still needed $1100 more than half of what she needed and the time was growing short. I have been in this sort of position myself, let me tell you who needs it! Being I always like to give in a way that makes a difference I told Britta I would cover what she needed. That time of year I have to spend money on all kinds of seeds so I look too what Britta was doing as planting spiritual seeds and an investment in eternal life!

Matthew 6:19-34

19 "Don't hoard treasure down here where it gets eaten by moths and corroded by rust or–worse!– stolen by burglars. 20 Stockpile treasure in heaven, where it's safe from moth and rust and burglars. 21 It's obvious, isn't it? The place where your treasure is, is the place you will most want to be, and end up being. 22 "Your eyes are windows into your body. If you open your eyes wide in wonder and belief, your body fills up with light. 23 If you live squinty-eyed in greed and distrust, your body is a dank cellar. If you pull the blinds on your windows, what a dark life you will have! 24 "You can't worship two gods at once. Loving one god, you'll end up hating the other. Adoration of one feeds contempt for the other. You can't worship God and Money both. 25 "If you decide for God, living a life of God-worship, it follows that you don't fuss about what's on the table at mealtimes or whether the clothes in your closet are in fashion. There is far more to your life than the food you put in your stomach, more to your outer appearance than the clothes you hang on your body. 26 Look at the birds, free and unfettered, not tied down to a

job description, careless in the care of God. And you count far more to him than birds. 27 "Has anyone by fussing in front of the mirror ever gotten taller by so much as an inch? 28 All this time and money wasted on fashion–do you think it makes that much difference? Instead of looking at the fashions, walk out into the fields and look at the wildflowers. They never primp or shop, 29 but have you ever seen color and design quite like it? The ten best-dressed men and women in the country look shabby alongside them. 30 "If God gives such attention to the appearance of wildflowers–most of which are never even seen–don't you think he'll attend to you, take pride in you, do his best for you? 31 What I'm trying to do here is to get you to relax, to not be so preoccupied with getting, so you can respond to God's giving. 32 People who don't know God and the way he works fuss over these things, but you know both God and how he works. 33 Steep your life in God-reality, God-initiative, God-provisions. Don't worry about missing out. You'll find all your everyday human concerns will be met. 34 "Give your entire attention to what God is doing right now, and don't get worked up about what may or may not happen tomorrow. God will help you deal with whatever hard things come up when the time comes.

I prefer to send money orders these days, anyone who knows my history, also knows I once had money troubles and tended to spend more than I had. You can't do that with money orders as you need to have the money to buy them! I sent Britta 2 of them for $550 each, hoping that they would encourage her in the ministry she was doing. For the past couple years Britta and I have kept in touch mostly by emails. After I had gotten most of my pumpkins planted on the 6th of June I took my Dad down to see his cousins in Illinois I got back early in the afternoon of the 10th I got on my computer and there was an update from Britta dated the day I left for Illinois here it is in part

Mike Kroll is the man who is in charge of financial support at camp and he recently informed me that the money order from you issued to my CRU account never reached his apartment. He is the one who officially deposits it into my camp account.

I want to ask you if you would consider issuing a new money order and sending it to me here at camp. If the original money order shows up in the mail, I will dispose of it. It would also be a good idea to cancel the original money order in case the envelope was stolen in the mail system.

If you are willing to issue a new money order, my address here at camp is:

Britta Lahr
Deer Creek Christian Camp
228 S Pine Dr.
Bailey, CO 80421


Praying and trusting that the Lord will resolve this issue with the lost mail. Thank you so much again, George, for everything. Hope to hear from you soon!

-Britta

Poor Britta I thought she is probably beside herself! I immediately emailed her back here it is in part

Hey Britta!

Great to hear from you! I will look for that money order stub and see if I can get another issued for you a.s.a.p.! I think I sent two one for 600 and one for five they are a little different than checks as you have to have the cash to get another and I am borrowing from my neighbor/friend to see me through till I get a crop thanks to all this wonderful rain this spring! So I don't really have any more ready cash available. It doesn't look like that will be for another month! You may want to pray that I find them as my book keeping is probably not the best in the world, but I know I put them somewhere! I am pretty sure that they won't put you out into the street Britta! Ha ha I will do all I can on my part to get you this as soon as possible! I just got home from Illinois so I will try finding them and let you know what I find out! If we can't get them replaced I will try and find 1100 dollars some place so don't worry Britta ok!

~George

I couldn't find those money order stubs anywhere! And believe me I had practically tore the whole place apart looking for them. I was in thought that I sent that money for Britta's ministry and it was probably very hard to concentrate on what she was doing down there thinking of all of this I opened my billfold up there was $1200 to live on till some kind of crop came in and it was borrowed money besides! At that time this scripture shot through my head!

John 15:13

13 This is the very best way to love. Put your life on the line for your friends.

I figured I should listen what Jesus was telling me and see how he would work it all out! I went and purchased 2 more money orders and sent them to Britta! 3 things happened almost immediately! I got home from sending off the money orders to Britta when there in my mail box was a letter from another friend from camp Kevin Ford. I had been in touch with Kevin for about a week he was going to borrow me $1000 until after camp sometime he said he really wasn't worried when I would pay it back, but instead of $1000 dollars her sent me $2000 later I asked Kevin why he had sent more, he told me while he was writing the check out he thought $1000 doesn't go very far these days! I paid Kevin back when I saw him at the Dells in late September the theme for this year was engage! The next day I was at one of my organic farms I stopped to talk with Doris, she is 1/3 partner with her 2 daughters on ownership of this land. I was telling Doris that her 2 daughters wanted the spring rent $6300 paid by July 1, but the way the year was this seemed impossible! Doris said without hesitation I'll borrow you the money George! Get in the car and let's go to the bank! I told Doris if those 2 daughters of hers ever found out she borrowed me the money they would have a fit! Doris said that was just too bad because they weren't going to get a thing after she was gone! While we were at the bank my cell phone rang it was Ann Kruse wondering if I could do something with their farm yet. I told Ann I would go over and look at her farm and give her a call as soon as I was done with my business with Doris, Ann said "be sure to tell Doris I said hi." Ann and Doris were once neighbors when the Kruse's and Doris lived in Mankato! I couldn't help peeking at Doris's balance in her savings account $160,000! You see it pays to have young friends as well as old friends young one's have the energy if you need that, and old ones tend to have money if you need that, I have neither so people are just out of luck if they need those 2 things from me! All I could say is God bless your heart Doris I paid her back after oat harvest she said she did want any interest ether. Doris also borrowed me $9400 interest free to plant my alfalfa crop over there for next year, but that's another story! After I talked with Doris I went and walked over the Kruse farm it was all overgrown with weeds waist high I called Ann and told her I could plow it yet and plant pumpkins yet I told Ann if I came out I would pay her some sort of rent. In the end it was a good thing I had those extra acres of pumpkins or I would have been severely short of what was needed! I told Ann several weeks back I would give her $2000 rent over there she was very happy and said she was only figuring on $500 as late as it was planted, half of that amount is paid, still waiting for some guys to pay me for hay, so I can pay the rest! Britta sure seemed worried about the missing money orders, but I had so much good fortune after I sent her those second money orders that I really didn't care if they ever showed up! I told Britta if they did to just go ahead and us it in her ministry down there! Britta sent me a letter after that explaining that God was showing her a lot through this ordeal! I was glad that God had used me to help out a friend in need, and was also glad that I listened to God in the first place! I pretty much made up my mind that those money orders were gone for good, so why bother with them anymore! I was looking forward to seeing Britta at camp in a couple weeks, but when camp time came Britta seemed like she was trying to avoid me. This was something that kind of hurt. Women! Why do I even try to be friends with them anyway? I made up my mind that I would cease emailing Britta after this! After I came home from camp I had so much work staring me in the face! People who I had lined up to take care of things while I was gone didn't have them done they let me down, and Monday the day after I returned it just had to rain! I don't know why I was digging through my dresser drawer, but those money orders were the furthest things from my mind! What just sort of popped out ate me, but those money order stubs! I wasn't doing anything that day because of the rain, so I went to the post office. I figured it should be an easy process to find out what happened to them but 45 minutes and $11.50 later the post office lady said I would receive compensation in the mail if the things hadn't been cashed. Then I went home and broke my promise to myself I emailed Britta telling her she would never believe what I found, the money order stubs, and my experience at the post office! Britta emailed back later that day with some wild news! Telling me that the ministry in Colorado had just contacted her and the money orders had just arrived that very day! She was just going to email me but I had beaten her to it with my news! I'm sorry but this is all too intricate to be just circumstance! It has God's finger prints all over it.

Ecclesiastes 11:5
5 Just as you'll never understand the mystery of life forming in a pregnant woman, So you'll never understand the mystery at work in all that God does.

After a few days I got reimbursed for the money orders from the government as I remember it came at a needy time. After a few more days Britta sent me the un cashed money orders but they were no longer valid. I mentioned earlier that I asked Britta to help me write this story and share her experience of the money order ordeal and here it is!

9/7/13

This past spring of 2013 I sent out an armful of letters to friends and family to raise money and prayer support for missions that God had for me. This would be the second summer of missions that I would be doing in the mountains of Colorado. The work is to share the story of Jesus with youth from inner city, Denver.

One of the people who supported me is my friend George Denn. George supported me financially both years I went, providing for nearly half of the total that was needed (not a small sum of cash!) It feels like there is no amount of "thank you" to say to someone who treats you with extravagant generosity.

Shortly before leaving for my trip, I sent off the envelope of the money orders from George praying that they would make it safe and sound to the ministry headquarters. A few weeks later…I heard that the money orders were lost in the mail. Floating in space, I supposed. Or sitting in some random person's wallet. Neither of these sounded like good options.

I was with my friends in Denver when I got the news the money orders were lost in the mail. Instead of becoming frantic, my friends helped me and told me that mail often gets held up due to Memorial Day. Still, I just had the feeling that they were not going to reach their destination. Once I told George about this, he generously sent me a new set of money orders. He had now supported me for double the original amount.

Weeks later there was still no sign of the original money orders. George misplaced the stubs, so he could not get the cash back that he already paid. And the tangible money orders were lost (basically the equivalent to losing cash in the mail).

I was not sure how to handle the situation. Should I refuse George's additional money and pay for the remainder of the summer out of pocket? Should I try to raise more money while I was already working on missions? Honestly, I had no idea what to do. I was angry at God, blaming Him for the lost money orders. I was also angry at myself, feeling like it was my fault as well. I felt very guilty and like I should not accept the money orders.

But Jesus came to me and spoke through friends. God was in control of the situation. He knew exactly where the original money orders were. God also knew that I would feel guilty and wanted to teach me a far greater lesson…about His love and grace. This situation parallels God's grace so beautifully. Jesus did not have to give His life, but chose to die on the cross out of love and generosity. George did not have to give the money, but he chose to trust God and give.

I had to swallow my pride and accept a generous, undeserved money gift from George.

1 and a half months after the missions in Colorado concluded, those original money orders appeared in the mail. The exactly same day as the tangible money orders appeared, George's stubs for the originals appeared as well.

"For my thoughts are not your thoughts, neither are your ways my ways," declares the LORD." –

Isaiah 55:8

-Britta Lahr

Many thanks Britta for helping me write this story, and also thanks for your friendship it does mean a lot to me! So what is God up to with all of this? Who knows maybe he just wanted a story written that glorifies him! And like Pilate said in John 19:22 I to have to say, what I have written, I have written!

Gods' abundant blessings to you all!

In Christ

George Denn

# Pumpkin picking survivor man! Or as the pumpkins were picked!

Ecclesiastes 7:14

14 In the day of prosperity be joyful, But in the day of adversity consider: Surely God has appointed the one as well as the other, So that man can find out nothing that will come after him.

This time of year I am bombarded with commercial grower seed catalogs, with pictures of many different varieties of pumpkins that one could order. Promising of exhalent crops and sales if I would just get my order in as early as possible, especially for certain new varieties! I have long come to see that my provision comes from the Lord, and any exhalent crop or sales probably comes from more of what he does, than anything I can do or buy! Before I start the task of ordering all the different varieties of pumpkin seeds I will need for next year's season I want to consider the season that has just past! I am still trying to make sense of it all! We all like to see God's grace and mercy and abundance in our lives, but what happens when he sends us a little adversity into our lives? Do we still see it as the hand of God? And what can we learn from such seasons? I don't know how much I have learned from the season just past, but here is a story of how God allowed some adversity to enter into my life.

This truly was a year of adversity! Too much rain in the spring on the heels of a year of drought. All my clover hay had winter killed all 111 acres of it. Which meant pretty much no income for me until way into July, but this year we were a month latter so make that August! People that I normally could count on seemed to let me down so when I came home from heartland camp I had a lot of extra work to do that I had expected to be done! By mid-August I was tired out, we were baling Oat straw one day the crop was bountiful, but the help was not! One day when I did scare up some help to stack and I could drive the baling tractor I was praying "God please send me some more help if I have to stack one more load of straw I think I am going to die!" Not too long after I said that prayer my cell phone was vibrating in my pocket. It was a guy who had worked for me in the past. Dylan asked, "George when are you going to be needing help this fall?" I said," how fast can you get out here?" "Do you mean like right now?" "Ya I mean like right now?" "Do I have a job for the season?" Dylan asked. "You have a job for the season" I said. Dylan had a friend Brandon that needed a Job also. I told Dylan to get here as soon as he could, and they both would have a job until the work was done in the fall. They were both there within half an hour! "Thank you Jesus for a prayer answered!" As I recall I also had others praying for workers to help me this fall. I was encouraged as I had about 5 more days of straw baling, 90 acres of rocks to pick up off some recently seeded alfalfa ground 60 acres of marsh hay to bale yet and 2 hay racks to build for my Eagle Lake pumpkin stand I had

2 weeks yet before I started to pick pumpkins but it generally takes about a week to get the signs all on the hay racks, and I needed my hay racks all freed up to do that. There was just too much work to do this year! Tracy Porter and Jordan came up on Labor Day weekend to help me get the stands put up. It was so hot that weekend I figured that was going to happen when we started out with such a cool August! I can honestly say that picking pumpkins in 100 degree heat is not my idea of having fun, but the job needed to commence! I have 61 days to market these pumpkins so there is not a lot of recreation time to be had within that time period! Poor Tracy with the combination of heat and the abundance of weeds in my first field to be picked sent his allergy's into hi gear! That field was the first one that I planted in the spring on the 22 of May The soil was still so cold at that time, it only had a 20% stand of pumpkins and the weeds were intense I had kept it clean as long as I could with cultivating but by the time I came home from Heartland camp the weeds had come practically solid with the pumpkins vining I had to let the field to fend for itself. I called it my experimental field I wanted to see how thin I could have pumpkins and still get a fair crop. In the end I got 50 loads of the biggest and best looking pumpkins off that 13 acre field, and I plowed about 10-20 ton of green manure via. Weeds back into the soil on September 22 exactly 4 months to the day it was planted! What God had taught me through that field this year that was through adversity fruit is born! After each stand was put up we got 4 put up that weekend. I had us all say a prayer over them and Tracy anointed us and the stands with oil. Even Dylan and Brandon were anointed, although they seemed very apprehensive to the whole idea! So we were all anointed for this "Ministry of Joy" that lay ahead. I was to realize latter that it wasn't my joy God was

necessarily concerned about! After Tracy and Jordan left I had to cut some hay that afternoon, but ended up cutting my right arm on the mowing machine. I had to call David Maki to come and get me where I was. I was bleeding pretty bad and needed to doctor it up. I got the bleeding stopped and made a bandage, but I have a 2 inch scar on my right arm, another farmer's battle wound! 2 brothers Andrew and Josh joined my pumpkin picking crew on the next morning. I know their father He had spoken to me about them working a few days earlier. Ashley Block came to work for her second year. Ashley is a distant relative of mine! She likes to tell everyone that we are related, she is my 3 cousins daughter on mothers side so it is pretty distant! I like teasing Ashley and often pay her in change! I'd say, "Ashley there is a lot of change coming to your life!" Ashley is 19 and a very good sport when it comes to my trying to be funny! I also got a call that morning from a guy named Keith asking if he could come to work, and stay at my place. I knew Keith from my early Days in Worldwide Church of God I haven't seen him since he graduated from high school 12 years ago he was now 30 and twice as big as I. Another Keith started on Wednesday he is a nephew of my friend Terry. By Friday Andrew and Josh were tired of the heat so they didn't come and didn't call. Their father called me latter to say he was sorry for his sons behavior and that Josh had almost died that day from an over dose of prescription drugs! Josh did call me latter the next week asking for a second chance. I really didn't want to but after I thought long and hard about it, because of his father's friend-ship, and I figured Jesus would want me to give him a second chance. I told Josh right to his face the only reason I was giving him another chance was because of my friendship with his father, and if it hap-pened again just don't come back. After that Josh got the nickname

Oklahoma from the rest of the pickers Josh is originally from Oklahoma. Josh was the one in the group that really surprised me I didn't figure he would last through the week, but he came every day after that, and I had practically no issues with him after that. In the end I had to tell him that I hadn't expected him to make it a week, let alone the end of the season, I had been wrong about him! He asked if he could work for me next season I told him he could, but Josh is 22 years old and I hope he finds something steady before then I gave him a $300 bonus and 3 of my books and shook his hand Josh amazed me! I and Keith no. 1 took 2 pickups and trailers loaded with pumpkins down to Spring Valley that Friday. We were halfway there in a town by the name of Ellendale when we stopped for gas I noticed Keith's trailer hitch was almost busted clear off! We were directed to go to Al's body shop where they restore older vehicles and they welded our trailer right up! When I got back home that day I meet the group at my Elysian stand. They were telling me that the trailer had come unhooked from Dylan's pickup shearing off a stop sign! They all thought I would be mad, but I found it humorous, and was just glad no one was hurt! After everything was unloaded we headed for home. Ashley and Keith no. 2 were behind me, all of a sudden my phone was ringing it was Ashley. Apparently the axle and wheel on the trailer had come out and banged and bounced down the highway in front of them and just disappeared! We never did find it we walked on both sides of the road for a half a mile I assumed someone would find it when they were picking corn, but to my knowledge it was never found! What a strange day I had more problems with trailers in one day than all the years I had used them! The next day Keith No. 2 called and said he needed to talk to me. Apparently when the axle came out of the trailer and went bouncing down the highway in front of them it scared Keith no. 2 so bad that he quit. And that was the end of Keith no. 2 we all named that stretch of road the Keith no. 2 memorial highway for Keith's 3 days of picking pumpkins with us! This was sort of a relief for me, because I was going to have to tell him to watch his foul mouth so now I didn't have too! The next Monday Dylan had a couple more friends show up for work Red beard was one of the guys, and I forgot the other ones he only worked 2 days and wasn't very good any how! Red beard stayed on and for the rest of that week things went on without a hitch except a window that got broke, buy Brandon and this was after I had already spoke to them about throwing pumpkins! So I had to address the group a little stronger this time and I think they got the message this time! Ray and Denise Olson and grandsons Michael and Gabriel came to help the weekend of September 15. It was a welcome relief to work with people of like mind for a change. Red beard and Brandon were sick the next day and Dylan only came in the morning the three didn't show up or call for the rest of the week my hopes of getting down to the dells celebration the next week were fading fast. I had hoped Dylan would be the leader of this group while I was gone now even he wasn't working out! I hired Josiah about this time, he was part of the Kenyan group last year, this year there would be no Kenyans as they all kind of went their separate ways! I thought what should I do Lord these are the people you have sent, but they are not working out all that well. They smoke when I am not around disrespecting me and sometimes it is more than just tobacco! Now they don't even come! How can I operate this way? I had an avenue that I could call for some Mexican help, but I felt that would have been from me and not God I was pondering all these things that Saturday as I was unloading corn bundles down by the big tree at the end of the drive when a little pickup drove in and an older gentleman in his 70's in white tee shirt and bib overalls came up to talk I thought it kind of odd because he was wearing the same brand overall's I was and not many wear overalls anymore! He asked me "where I was hiding Dylan I'm his grandpa." "Dylan" I practically laughed, "has not been working since Monday," I said. "What!" said his grandfather almost in astonishment "let me give him a call." The man called Dylan said he was out here talking with George and he tells me that you haven't been to work since Monday! "I have a flat tire," Dylan said. "Pump it up!" Responded grandpa. "I've been sick," Said Dylan. "Take a pill!" said grandpa. Dylan told his grandpa that he had been fired. The old guy asked if I had fired Dylan "no but I would like to, but at this time I am so desperate for help all he has to do is show up!" Dylan hung up on his grandpa after he gave him some words of advice! "I'm sorry for all this George," the old guy said. "I feel responsible because I'm his grandpa" I assured the old guy it wasn't his fault I suspected Dylan was on some sort of drugs and he and Brandon was living down in a motel in north Mankato. I told the old guy "Dylan is not the same person he once was. Since he came home from the military he has changed and not in a good way!" The old guy left kind of dis heartened, and I went back to work. About 11 o'clock that day Dylan and Brandon came back to work. Perhaps Grandpa had some pull after all? Perhaps the pickup that belonged to his Grandpa that he had been driving had something to do with it? I was talking with Dylan a little later he told me that he had pneumonia. I was telling him of my conversation with his Grandpa. I told Dylan he had to be a good guy as he wore the same kind of bib overalls that I do! A puzzled look came over Dylan he told me that he has never known his Grandpa to wear bib overalls not ever! I started to think that I may have had a conversation with an angel!

Hebrews 13:2
Do not forget to entertain strangers, for by so doing some have unwittingly entertained angels.

Whether an angel or not the conversation I had with the old gentleman seemed to have had some connection with Dylan showing up so suddenly! Red beard also showed up that afternoon with his girlfriend Payton who I hired also. I let all of those who just came back to work know how disappointed I was, and how much they had cost me by not coming so I was unable to get the product out on the stands in a timely fashion! But now there was a glimmer of hope that I might be able to get to the Dells on Thursday. I pushed every one as hard as I could myself included, and was almost to the point of feeling confident I could go to the Dells and these people could handle things while I was gone, boy was I wrong! I left instructions what to do while I was gone, but before I could take in opening services I had received 2 phone calls from back home! Josiah had called me he seemed to be a little confused in who was running things and wondered if he could just wait until Monday to come back to work! I told him part of being a worker was to get along with those he was working with and that if he didn't come until Monday he might just as well stay home for good! The second call was from Keith telling of all the things that were going on back home things that were not good! Keith said they took a vote and voted Josiah off the Island! Personally I always got a kick out of Josiah! I once did have to tell him to just be quiet so I could have a few minutes to think about how to plan the day at hand. I did tell Keith and Dylan that if I had to come home to straighten things out that I would probably have to go to jail, because I would personally kill every one of them! I doubt that Jesus would have handled the situation that way, but I was tired of leaving these people for just few hours and every time they turn into the Keystone Cops! I left the Dells immediately after services were over on Sunday I turned on my phone and immediately there was a message for me from Larry Harbo, my apple guy stating he was very unhappy that he hadn't received his load of pumpkins yet, something that should have happened on Friday morning! I was on the phone from the time I drove onto hwy 90 at the Dells until I reached the Minnesota border trying to get things straightened out from the days I was gone I did get a hold of Red beard to get the load of pumpkins to Larry's that afternoon Apparently the person that was supposed to do this was scared that the truck would clunk out on him as it was running rough! It came to me the next week that this pumpkin business was all created over a period of years and I was the only one that could stock those stands in an efficient way! I came home from the Dells that afternoon to find Keith lying in front of my kitchen stove passed out drunk on the floor! "What am I going to do with these people Lord?" I knew I had to address this when the time was right Keith is about twice as big and half as old as I, so I didn't really relish the thought of confronting him but I knew I had too. I just had to wait for the right time! Fights seemed to be breaking out daily this week I asked David Maki if he would drive the vehicle with half the crew to go pick pie pumpkins, but Brandon got mad at David and a vocal fight broke out I went over and told Brandon he was threw working for me. Keith talked me into giving Brandon a second chance. The next day I got a call from Josh saying a fight was breaking out between Keith and Brandon I had sent those 3 to pick squash, and I took the rest of the crew to pick pie pumpkins for most of the morning there was no tension present until Josh called. Josh wondered what he should do I told Josh just to mind his own business and let the 2 pound the hell out of one another, and take whoever was left standing to go unload the squash! I really didn't know what else to say at the moment? I'm pretty sure that's not how Jesus would have handled the situation, but I was getting tired of this crew for lack of respect for one another and for me smoking and drinking when I was not present. Somehow Keith had talked Ashley into stopping at a liquor store on the way home. Ashley told me what happened, I told Ashley if he did it again just to drive off and leave him! When Jeff and I got home that night from collecting the money Keith was sleeping in my recliner chair in the kitchen. I was awakened that night around 2 AM too very load music and Keith hollering "George wake up!" several times he tried my door but I had it locked. He started banging on the low piano keys saying,"George you shity Christian wake up!" He then proceeded to break my door open! I started to call the cops but figured by the time they got there Keith would have my door busted down. I knew the time to confront Keith was here, or just cower to fear.

Romans 8:15

15 This resurrection life you received from God is not a timid, grave-tending life. It's adventurously expectant, greeting God with a childlike "What's next, Papa?"

I threw the door open and confronted Keith, and for the next 5 hours I had an argument with a drunk! David Maki came home from work around 7 am boy was I sure glad to see him! I told Keith that either he had to leave or I had to, because he was up all hours of the night arguing with his girlfriend or others on his phone, that I needed to be able to sleep so I could work the next day. Keith drank about a quart of whisky a day plus 16 beers His father was this way and died with liver poisoning at 45! Keith was 30 and if he don't quit soon he won't make it to be as old as his dad was! I told Keith that I was taking him to a bus stop and asked him if he had any money. He said he had $800. I told him that would get him anywhere in America except here! I also told Keith to do himself a favor and go to the first alcohol treatment center he could find and turn himself in. Last I heard from Keith it was obvious he didn't go with my suggestion! Keith talked a pretty good talk of God Jesus, and the Holy Spirit, but his drinking and lack of respect, and living with his girlfriend on weekends pretty much shows his fruits.

Matthew 7:15-20

15 "Beware of false prophets, who come to you in sheep's clothing, but inwardly they are ravenous wolves. 16 You will know them by their fruits. Do men gather grapes from thornbushes or figs from thistles? 17 Even so, every good tree bears good fruit, but a bad tree bears bad fruit. 18 A good tree cannot bear bad fruit, nor can a bad tree bear good fruit. 19 Every tree that does not bear good fruit is cut down and thrown into the fire. 20 Therefore by their fruits you will know them.

Then again anyone can change! For a few days everyone got along well. Then Brandon started fighting with Red beard. I told Brandon to leave Red beard alone because I didn't want any more fighting! Brandon started to remind me of the guy Jesus was talking about.

Matthew 18:23-35

23 "The kingdom of God is like a king who decided to square accounts with his servants. 24 As he got under way, one servant was brought before him who had run up a debt of a hundred thousand dollars. 25 He couldn't pay up, so the king ordered the man, along with his wife, children, and goods, to be auctioned off at the slave market. 26 "The poor wretch threw himself at the king's feet and begged, 'Give me a chance and I'll pay it all back.' 27 Touched by his plea, the king let him off, erasing the debt. 28 "The servant was no sooner out of the room when he came upon one of his fellow servants who owed him ten dollars. He seized him by the throat and demanded, 'Pay up. Now!' 29 "The poor wretch threw himself down and begged, 'Give me a chance and I'll pay it all back.' 30 But he wouldn't do it. He had him arrested and put in jail until the debt was paid. 31 When the other servants saw this going on, they were outraged and brought a detailed report to the king. 32 "The king summoned the man and said, 'You evil servant! I forgave your entire debt when you begged me for mercy. 33 Shouldn't you be compelled to be merciful to your fellow servant who asked for mercy?' 34 The king

was furious and put the screws to the man until he paid back his entire debt. 35 And that's exactly what my Father in heaven is going to do to each one of you who doesn't forgive unconditionally anyone who asks for mercy."

This Red beard and his girlfriend Payten were characters too! Red beard was 22 and Payten was 17. They lived together at the same motel Brandon and Dylan were staying at. I asked Payten one day how come she wasn't going to school. "Oh I'm taking a vacation from that," she said. I just couldn't believe it! Red beard came from a well-grounded Christian upbringing went to Christian school growing up and could talk about the Lord like the best of them, but behind my back he and Dylan would be smoking cigarettes as well as synthetic marijuana. He would lie about his and Payten's hours and twice I caught him stealing gas although once it was diesel fuel. That afternoon his truck was running poorly he said he must have gotten some bad gas! Hmm I wonder who put the jug of diesel fuel in their pickup. All my $2 bills were stolen from my bedroom I'm pretty sure it was Red beard, but I have no proof! All I knew what to do with this group was to pray for them daily, ask God why he sent these folks to me, and wonder how on earth we get as many pumpkins picked as we do it seemed we were getting more done each day than in years past this is the first time I couldn't wait for the season to be over! One day I was thinking of all these things. I was really discouraged walking to the mail box I was wondering why I just didn't disk down the rest of the pumpkins and tell everyone just to go home and be done with it! About that time these 2 happy little girls jumped out from behind one of the signs and hollered "Thanks mister for putting all these pumpkins out for us!"

Psalms 8:2
2 Out of the mouth of babes and nursing infants You
have ordained strength, Because of Your enemies,
That You may silence the enemy and the avenger.

I was encouraged greatly by these 2 girls it helped me to gain back my perspective why I was doing all this in the first place!

Like the weedy pumpkin field at the beginning of my story my squash field seemed to be telling me another story. Usually these things ripen fairly close together. Not this year I seemed to have 2 very distingue groups in the same field. Some were ripe and some were not I ended up picking the ripe ones and having to leave the un-ripe ones hoping that more time would ripen them. Just like God wishes for none of us to perish.

2 Peter 3:9
9 God isn't late with his promise as some measure
lateness. He is restraining himself on account of you,
holding back the End because he doesn't want anyone
lost. He's giving everyone space and time to change.

I didn't want any of these squash to perish as they were quite valuable to me if they would ripen. I had to smash some to get the ripe ones out of the field, but in the end they just wouldn't ripen and 1/3 of them did perish in the elements they ended up being plowed under and mixed with the soil. I was glad to have saved as many as

I could. One day I had 2 of my best pickups blow up within 1/2 hour of one another. I was able to get one of them going again, and was able to finish the season with it. I scrapped them both out and there back ends are ready to be made into trailers for next year.

The weekend of Oct 5 Tom and Sandy Kennebeck ventured down from Orr Mn to help do some picking and take back a trailer load of pumpkins for a youth fundraiser up there. Lynne Pahl and Grandson Nick as well as Denise Olson ventured up from Wisconsin on the next weekend. It always amazes me how quickly my house gets straightened out when there are women around they must have some sort of miraculous powers! On Sunday Rochester Church as well as Doug Johannsens 2 congregations were here from the Twin cities. we picked 20 loads of pumpkins and picked enough to load for the next week! We finished picking pumpkins on the 26 of October I could finally get back to having just 2 people working for the rest of the season! Doug Johannsen and Rick Shallenberger came out to go on the money run with me on Sunday the 27 neither of them had experienced anything like it! Dylan and Brandon kept working I still needed to have them help me with take down which takes about a week starting on November 1. I still had hay to put up and plowing to do, because I just let it go until pumpkin season was done, because the workers didn't seem to get much done unless I was Present! My workers seemed to me this year like Paul's thorn in the flesh was to him.

2 Corinthians 12:7-10

7 Because of the extravagance of those revelations, and so I wouldn't get a big head, I was given the gift of a handicap to keep me in constant touch with

my limitations. Satan's angel did his best to get me down; what he in fact did was push me to my knees. No danger then of walking around high and mighty! 8 At first I didn't think of it as a gift, and begged God to remove it. Three times I did that, 9 and then he told me, My grace is enough; it's all you need. My strength comes into its own in your weakness. Once I heard that, I was glad to let it happen. I quit focusing on the handicap and began appreciating the gift. It was a case of Christ's strength moving in on my weakness. 10 Now I take limitations in stride, and with good cheer, these limitations that cut me down to size–abuse, accidents, opposition, bad breaks. I just let Christ take over! And so the weaker I get, the stronger I become.

I didn't exactly rejoice in my limitations as Paul did, but like Paul God seemed to be saying that his Grace was sufficient for me as well! I got 80 acres of pumpkins picked with this crew, what a miracle that was! In spite of all the turmoil I had with these workers God sent me this year, some days I still scratch my head and wonder what God had in mind for myself as well as those he sent? However the Gospel had been preached! I don't know exactly how many books were given away this year, but I know I bought 1500 of them. Food was given to the poor as some of the notes that I received in my boxes attest to. Also sales of product were up 9% from the previous year, and I survived it all, so I will call it a successful year! I did get the rest of my hay put up 2 days before it snowed, and the field work got done before it froze up. At Thanksgiving time I drove down to

Wisconsin and dropped of a load of hay for some goats that Ray and Denise Olson have, then ventured on down to visit Tracy Porter and family. I returned home the next week and found one of my work trucks had been stolen! I put it in God's hands and called the cops. It was retrieved in 2 days unscathed! I was probably more concerned about the tools I had left in it than the truck, but they too seemed to be all intact!

So as this year fades and another is about to begin here is something to consider the past, as well as the future!

> Psalm 145
>
> 1 I lift you high in praise, my God, O my King! and I'll bless your name into eternity. 2 I'll bless you every day, and keep it up from now to eternity. 3 God is magnificent; he can never be praised enough. There are no boundaries to his greatness. 4 Generation after generation stands in awe of your work; each one tells stories of your mighty acts. 5 Your beauty and splendor have everyone talking; I compose songs on your wonders. 6 Your marvelous doings are headline news; I could write a book full of the details of your greatness. 7 The fame of your goodness spreads across the country; your righteousness is on everyone's lips. 8 God is all mercy and grace—not quick to anger, is rich in love. 9 God is good to one and all; everything he does is suffused with grace. 10 Creation and creatures applaud you, God; 11 your holy people bless you. They talk about the glories of your rule, they exclaim over your splendor, 12

Letting the world know of your power for good, the lavish splendor of your kingdom. 13 Your kingdom is a kingdom eternal; you never get voted out of office. God always does what he says, and is gracious in everything he does. 14 God gives a hand to those down on their luck, gives a fresh start to those ready to quit. 15 All eyes are on you, expectant; you give them their meals on time. 16 Generous to a fault, you lavish your favor on all creatures. 17 Everything God does is right–the trademark on all his works is love. 18 God's there, listening for all who pray, for all who pray and mean it. 19 He does what's best for those who fear him–hears them call out, and saves them. 20 God sticks by all who love him, but it's all over for those who don't. 21 My mouth is filled with God's praise. Let everything living bless him, bless his holy name from now to eternity!

I guess I will go and order those pumpkin seeds for next year now, and see where it all takes me!

Happy new year to you all!

in Christ,

George Denn

# Hey By George! April 7 2014

# CHANGING SEASONS

Act's:6-8

**6** Therefore, when they had come together, they asked Him, saying, "Lord, will You at this time restore the kingdom to Israel?" **7** And He said to them, "It is not for you to know times or seasons which the Father has put in His own authority. **8** But you shall receive power when the Holy Spirit has come upon you; and you shall be witnesses to Me in Jerusalem, and in all Judea and Samaria, and to the end of the earth."

Today I declared spring has arrived on my farm! This is traditionally done here by me by opening the double doors on my machine shed. But unlike other years instead of a nice clean place I was met by a giant mess! It was one that I had created last fall by just putting everything in there that I felt needed to be picked up and put under a roof before it snowed; which happened abruptly 2 days after I closed the shed doors for the winter! One of the first things I try to do once we get some snow, is to take my skid loader and push snow up against my old house. This makes great insulation and is free for the taking! It stops drafts on the floors and keeps my water pipes from freezing, when temperatures in Minnesota drop to -0 degrees! My 2 wood stoves that are affectionately named by my longtime friend Terry Tricky. The one in the kitchen he calls hellfire and the one in the basement damnation. He called them this as he has witnessed me put everything one could imagine to the flame and some things you probably couldn't imagine! Everything is purified through hellfire and damnation he stated! Someone asked me one time how much wood it took to heat my house through the winter. 15 full sized pickup loads with side boards, it takes a lot of wood to heat a corn crib was my answer! The guy just laughed but I was dead serious, however that does keep the place at a balmy 75-80 degrees when the fires are going. Usually there are coals still hot in the morning that re-kindle a fire. I generally don't put any wood on the fires after 9 in the evening. Every morning I do what I call the morning ritual which is, I get up to sometimes a very cold house fill the stoves with wood, If there are no hot coals I splash on some diesel fuel and strike a match. In no time at all the cold kitchen turns into a nice warm room, by this time the morning coffee is done so I pour a cup and sit down into my recliner next to the stove, were I read, pray, or fall asleep which-ever comes first! Wood heat is such a comforting, inviting form of heat that I find it hard to go visiting in the winter. Most people keep their thermostat at near 65 degrees to save on fuel. I don't blame them I would do the same. I am used to 75- 80 so I tend to freeze! I was talking to my land lady Doris last winter. Doris was telling me that her heat bill for January was $1100 and she could only have her house 55 degrees, because propane prices were over $5 a gallon. I know others that didn't get their fire wood cut early and the snow got so deep it was almost impossible to get to any. I too have learned from hardship to get my firewood cut in the springtime so when I'm done in the fall I don't have that job to do. I have a motto about fire wood it is free, but it isn't cheap. Just the other day I was out sawing a dead tree down, when it fell the butt jumped up and hit me under the jaw and knocked out a couple of fillings.

Ecclesiastes 10:9
And he who splits wood may be endangered by it.

So there are the hidden costs associated with firewood, and I am sure my dentist Bryan will fix me right up! One cold weekend in early December Rick Bengston came for a visit. It got down to -20 below zero , and one of my chimney caps were frosting up, so when the wind would blow it blew the smoke down the chimney, and smoked up the house! Rick had one of his window washing poles and a brush with so we set up a ladder and he was able to get the frost brushed off. I usually take those caps off for the winter, because of that reason but alas my procrastinating ways finally caught up with me! About 3 weeks later this happened again. This time I took my 22 rifle and shot at the chimney cap! This worked fine every couple hours I would go out and shot at the chimney cap, until one night the gun mis-fired and blew some pieces off my gun! I could no longer keep the cap un-frosted so I finally had to call a friend who has a boom truck so he could lift me up and I could take the caps off. The morning we did this I thought I would clean out the chimney in the basement. I had to put on one of my winter gloves, because when I stuck my hand in there I could feel a fire had already been smoldering in the chimney. I also ran a brush down the chimney while I was up there on the boom truck the chimney had been pretty much plugged! After all of this I could see that God had protected me from having a chimney fire and possibly burning down the house!

Psalm 54:6-7

**6** I'm ready now to worship, so ready. I thank you, God–you're so good. **7** You got me out of every scrape, and I saw my enemies get it.

Winter is a time when I don't do a whole lot. I get my seeds ordered, do my taxes and take life easy! As nice as it is to have nothing much to do all winter after a couple of months it does get old. This winter I had the opportunity to winter near Orlando Florida, but the guys who bought hay from me were so slow to pay me I never got there I guess it wasn't in Gods' plan that I do that!

Proverbs 16:9 A man's heart plans his way, but the Lord directs his steps.

In mid-January I did get up to Snow Blast, it was held near Virginia MN this year. It was good to get away for a weekend and visit with old friends. Near the end of February I went down to camp training near Peoria Ill. Before I left I told David Maki not to let the house play tricks on him while I was gone, he just laughed! I took my dad to Cousin Nancy's place near Momence Ill, while I went to camp training. I saw a lot of new faces so it looks like the make-up of camp is changing again this happens about every 3 years or so new people come, some that have been there awhile leave and so changes the make-up of camp. When I got home the whole house smelled strongly of wood smoke! I asked David what in the world went on while I was gone. He was telling me that my chimney must be clogged as the whole house just filled up with smoke. It was fairly cold with just the one stove going. I investigated the chimney it seemed to be drawing ok. I lit the stove somehow the damper had closed tight I opened it some and was just fine. I told this to David he couldn't believe it was that simple! I just laughed this old house seems to have a personality all its own that's why I told him what I did before I left. I've been here for 52 years now so I know most of its tricks! Last fall my friend Tracy Porter had given me 2 books to read on healing. By the first of March I had those both read. One day in early March my sister Jane called telling me that our sister Marie who lives in Terrebonne Oregon had a stroke and a double brain aneurysm at that point her chances of making it through this was pretty bleak! I had been thinking of Marie for a couple of weeks, and remembering what the authors of the books said, that Jesus was ultimately the only one that could truly heal. I resolved to pray and asked others to pray for Marie as well. I am happy to write that I called Marie today and we were able to have a phone conversation she is in rehab for a couple more weeks in Portland Oregon.

Isaiah 30:26

**26** Moreover the light of the moon will be as the light of the sun, And the light of the sun will be sevenfold, As the light of seven days, In the day that the Lord binds up the bruise of His people And heals the stroke of their wound.

Around the 20th of March I went to Converge East somewhere in Eastern Ohio. I went with Josh, Rick, and Troy. Troy is one of the pastors from GCI in Rochester MN. Converge is for those involved in youth ministry. In the past I did not go to this, because I felt my motives for wanting to go were wrong. I am not doing much in youth ministry anymore except being a chaperone or working on security. So I would go to such an advent just to converse with old friends! Troy said "George you're not doing anything anyway so you should come with us, besides it won't cost you anything! So that is why I went because Troy talked me into it! I guess God wanted me to go to this because, Tracy Porter also asked if I wanted to drive down to his place and go to Converge with him and Cheri. I was encouraged to see all the young people there excited with their walk with Jesus Christ, and looking forward to serve at the camps! One evening at dinner I was talking to a young woman named Britney. She was telling me that she was going to collage to be a teacher, and would take part in the camp in Ohio for the first time. In the course of conversation I learned she liked to garden. I told her that I raised 80 acres of pumpkins. Britney said she didn't have much luck with pumpkins as the wild turkeys would eat the seeds. It just impressed me to meet a young person who liked to garden I don't know many who do. I also mentioned to Britney that camp would change her life, it sure did mine it probably was the best thing I ever did. I always say you can't send a youth to camp without it changing them, and you can't go yourself without it changing you! They said at the end of converge that we would leave with something that we hadn't come with. I left being encouraged that there were a lot of young people out there with a strong faith in Jesus, so in the end I was glad I went! On the third of April my Pastor friend Gordy from Duluth MN and I drove down to Chicago. We were heading to the GCI district church conference, another great weekend to fellowship with old and new friends! I was noticing on our journey a lot of things were not as they seemed. The next day our pastor general gave a message and one of his points was that things are not always as they seem! The theme for the weekend was sharing Jesus' faith love and hope. I came away with a greater understanding that even if I don't seem to possess these gifts in abundance I needn't worry because Jesus has plenty of faith hope and love to go around! It is not up to me to muster these things up within myself. Another thing I noticed that there were a lot of father- daughters and father- sons attending more so than any other conference I have attended. This too was an encouragement it reminded me of the scripture in Malachi.

> Malachi 4:6
> **6** And he will turn The hearts of the fathers to the children, And the hearts of the children to their fathers, Lest I come and strike the earth with a curse."

It is like I returned home to a new season, almost all the snow is gone, and the lake is starting to open up. Soon it will be planting season once again! The big mess in the shed is somewhat smaller I started a fire and burned what I could, the rest I will get at that another time. I have 4 more loads of wood to get cut so I will be done shortly with next winter's fuel needs! So this fall when the work is all done once again I can kick back in my recliner near the wood stove and not fear what it says in the proverbs!

proverbs 26:20

Where there is no wood the fire goes out;

God's peace and abundant blessings to you all!

Your brother in Christ,

George Denn

## Hey by George! June 1 2014

# THE UNUSUAL SPRING!

Hebrews 6:7

For the earth which drinks in the rain that often comes upon it, and bears herbs useful for those by whom it is cultivated, receives blessing from God;

It seemed as if spring would never get here this year! Around mid-April it looked as if I could prepare some ground to plant oats on, but the frost was not out of the ground yet. After sitting around all winter I was ready to get back to work. I worked up 33 acres on April 15 to be seeded to Oats the next day. The next day dawned cold and cloudy with a 90% chance of rain mixed with snow predicted!

Many things past through my head that morning as I had to fight the comfort of my wood stove, which beckoned to me to don't go out at all, stay here where it is warm in your nice recliner chair and drink coffee instead! "Do as much as you can when you can!" came a warning from a neighbor from many years ago. I was thinking of that scripture from Ecclesiastes.

Ecclesiastes 11:4

He who observes the wind will not sow, And he who regards the clouds will not reap.

I wasn't sure what to do I needed wisdom from the Lord!

James 1:2-7

Consider it a sheer gift, friends, when tests and challenges come at you from all sides. **3** You know that under pressure, your faith-life is forced into the open and shows its true colors. **4** So don't try to get out of anything prematurely. Let it do its work so you become mature and well-developed, not deficient in any way. **5** If you don't know what you're doing, pray to the Father. He loves to help. You'll get his help, and won't be condescended to when you ask for it. **6** Ask boldly, believingly, without a second thought. People who "worry their prayers" are like wind-whipped waves. **7** Don't think you're going to get anything from the Master that way

So after some prayer even though I would have rather stayed in the house that day I decided I needed to step out on faith that day and see how far that would take me!

James 2:14-26

Dear friends, do you think you'll get anywhere in this if you learn all the right words but never do anything? Does merely talking about faith indicate that a person really has it? **15** For instance, you come upon an old friend dressed in rags and half-starved **16** and say, "Good morning, friend! Be clothed in Christ! Be filled with the Holy Spirit!" and walk off without providing so much as a coat or a cup of soup–where does that get you? **17** Isn't it obvious that God-talk without God-acts is outrageous nonsense? **18** I can already hear one of you agreeing by saying "Sounds good. You take care of the faith department; I'll handle the works department." Not so fast. You can no more show me your works apart from your faith than I can show you my faith apart from my works. Faith and works, works and faith, fit together hand in glove. **19** Do I hear you professing to believe in the one and only God, but then observe you complacently sitting back as if you had done something wonderful? That's just great. Demons do that, but what good does it do them? **20** Use your heads! Do you suppose for a minute that you can cut faith and works in two and not end up with a corpse on your hands? **21** Wasn't our ancestor Abraham "made right with God by works" when he placed his son Isaac on the sacrificial altar? **22** Isn't it obvious that faith and works are yoked partners, that faith expresses itself in works? That the works are "works of faith"? **23** The full meaning of "believe" in the Scripture sentence, "Abraham believed God and was set right with God," includes his action. It's that mesh of believing and acting that got Abraham named "God's friend." **24** Is it not evident that a person is made right with God not by a barren faith but by faith fruitful in works? **25** The same with Rahab, the Jericho harlot. Wasn't her action in hiding God's spies and helping them escape–that seamless unity of believing and doing–what counted with God? **26** The very moment you separate body and spirit, you end up with a corpse. Separate faith and works and you get the same thing: a corpse.

I went to get the wagon load of Oats that I saved for seed last summer. That was keep dry all this time sitting in Doris's shed. It started to sprinkle before I got to the field, but I filled the 60 bushel hopper on the grain drill and started seeding my first field. I loaded the drill again and did my second field. For the third time that day I filled the drill, and started seeding my last field it was misting pretty good by the time I had finish for the day! 15 inches of snow had fallen that day as I planted Oats 70 miles north of where I was and it was raining pretty good by the time I got the wagon load of Oats back to the shed. I could see how the Lord had helped me out that day, as far as I knew I was the only person out in the field in these parts that day! This year my birthday April 20 fell on Easter Sunday. I turned 52 that day and was feeling every inch of it! Every year it seems like there are new aches and pains I didn't have before! Wayne Schwartz invited me over for supper that day. Anne Kruse was our cook; Joe and David Kruse were there too! Joe and David worked for me once upon a time! David is now in seminary someday he will be a Catholic priest and Joe is home for a short time from Italy he is a Friar now which means brother. I was the only Protestant in the bunch! We had a few days at that point with no rain and farmer that I am I couldn't help but look at one of my fields while I was at Wayne's that day and determined that the next Day I would work up the 33 acres over there. I got the Oats planted on the 22 of April and it was about the last day until May sometime that the ground could be worked! That next weekend I drove to Milwaukee and back and only saw two fields of corn planted the entire way! My Tractor had been in the shop twice this spring since March I got it home just in time to start preparing the ground for planting pumpkins. Danielle Lahr a young friend of mine from Eau Claire Wis. had e-mailed me back in March that her and some friends from the Raffa house would like to come and help plant Pumpkins this spring after various e-mails it was determined that the time that would work for them to come would only work out for Danielle so she came by herself on Saturday evening on Memorial day weekend. I was going to start Plowing ground on Monday morning the week before we would plant but decided to start a day sooner. I got a flat tire on one of the big rear tractor tires around 5 pm and had to quit until I could hopefully get a repair man out the next morning! My neighbor David came over for coffee shortly after I got home he told me that is what I get for working on Sunday! I told David I had heard that statement all my life and didn't believe God operated that way and was viewing God in an in accurate way! I told David that I had given my life to Jesus long ago my work is for him not me everything I have is his, not mine! David Maki was there and I kindly asked David as an impartial person in this discussion to read us at this time Romans 14 if he would!

Romans 14
Welcome with open arms fellow believers who don't
see things the way you do. And don't jump all over

them every time they do or say something you don't agree with–even when it seems that they are strong on opinions but weak in the faith department. Remember, they have their own history to deal with. Treat them gently. **2** For instance, a person who has been around for a while might well be convinced that he can eat anything on the table, while another, with a different background, might assume all Christians should be vegetarians and eat accordingly. **3** But since both are guests at Christ's table, wouldn't it be terribly rude if they fell to criticizing what the other ate or didn't eat? God, after all, invited them both to the table. **4** Do you have any business crossing people off the guest list or interfering with God's welcome? If there are corrections to be made or manners to be learned, God can handle that without your help. **5** Or, say, one person thinks that some days should be set aside as holy and another thinks that each day is pretty much like any other. There are good reasons either way. So, each person is free to follow the convictions of conscience. **6** What's important in all this is that if you keep a holy day, keep it for God's sake; if you eat meat, eat it to the glory of God and thank God for prime rib; if you're a vegetarian, eat vegetables to the glory of God and thank God for broccoli. **7** None of us are permitted to insist on our own way in these matters. **8** It's God we are answerable to–all the way from life to death and everything in between–not each other. **9** That's why Jesus lived and died and then lived again:

so that he could be our Master across the entire range of life and death, and free us from the petty tyrannies of each other. **10** So where does that leave you when you criticize a brother? And where does that leave you when you condescend to a sister? I'd say it leaves you looking pretty silly–or worse. Eventually, we're all going to end up kneeling side by side in the place of judgment, facing God. Your critical and condescending ways aren't going to improve your position there one bit. **11** Read it for yourself in Scripture: "As I live and breathe," God says, "every knee will bow before me; Every tongue will tell the honest truth that I and only I am God." **12**So tend to your knitting. You've got your hands full just taking care of your own life before God. **13**Forget about deciding what's right for each other. Here's what you need to be concerned about: that you don't get in the way of someone else, making life more difficult than it already is. **14** I'm convinced–Jesus convinced me!–that everything as it is in itself is holy. We, of course, by the way we treat it or talk about it, can contaminate it. **15** If you confuse others by making a big issue over what they eat or don't eat, you're no longer a companion with them in love, are you? These, remember, are persons for whom Christ died. Would you risk sending them to hell over an item in their diet? **16** Don't you dare let a piece of God-blessed food become an occasion of soul-poisoning! **17** God's kingdom isn't a matter of what you put in your stomach, for goodness' sake. It's what God does with your life as he sets it right, puts it together, and completes it with joy. **18**Your task is to single-mindedly serve Christ. Do that and you'll kill two birds with one stone: pleasing the God above you and proving your worth to the people around you. **19** So let's agree to use all our energy in getting along with each other. Help others with encouraging words; **20**don't drag them down by finding fault. You're certainly not going to permit an argument over what is served or not served at supper to wreck God's work among you, are you? I said it before and I'll say it again: All food is good, but it can turn bad if you use it badly, if you use it to trip others up and send them sprawling. **21** When you sit down to a meal, your primary concern should not be to feed your own face but to share the life of Jesus. So be sensitive and courteous to the others who are eating. Don't eat or say or do things that might interfere with the free exchange of love. **22**Cultivate your own relationship with God, but don't impose it on others. You're fortunate if your behavior and your belief are coherent. **23** But if you're not sure, if you notice that you are acting in ways inconsistent with what you believe–some days trying to impose your opinions on others, other days just trying to please them–then you know that you're out of line. If the way you live isn't consistent with what you believe, then it's wrong.

I am convinced in my mind that there are no special days that Jesus Christ is our Sabbath. I called the tire place the next morning and they came right out it was rainy that day but not enough to stop me from plowing another day I was the only one out in the field in these parts! Later that day I was over to David's we were drinking coffee when his wife Darcy came home from work. She asked David if he had gotten anything done that day. He told her that he had been at my place that morning having coffee and then it rained so he didn't do anything that day. I told Darcy I had finished my plowing! She told David "work before pleasure Gibson, No wonder you're not getting anything done! I thought it a humorous moment after he gave me the business the day before for working on Sunday! Later that week I was disking down what I had plowed and a hanger for the bearing broke about the same time I noticed that the alternator light had come on in the tractor. I checked the alternator it was still fine just not charging. Normally when it goes on this tractor sparks are flying and it gives off a smell of metal and belts burning! I hoped I could finish what I was doing for next I would be working at Wayne's he is my on staff mechanic as well as my Land lord! Wayne keeps my junk fixed up so I had a few things for him to repair when I got moved back over there! I plowed on Thursday and was disking on Friday I could hear and smell the alternator go on the tractor so I had to stop and go 20 miles too Smiths Mill Implement and get a new one $220 and 20 miles later I was back in business I sure was glad that guy who owed me for some hay had paid me yesterday! My needs had been covered for that day.

Matthew 6:31-34

What I'm trying to do here is to get you to relax, to not be so preoccupied with getting, so you can respond to God's giving. **32** People who don't know God and the way he works fuss over these things, but you know both God and how he works. **33** Steep your life in God-reality, God-initiative, God-provisions. Don't worry about missing out. You'll find all your everyday human concerns will be met. **34** "Give your entire attention to what God is doing right now, and don't get worked up about what may or may not happen tomorrow. God will help you deal with whatever hard things come up when the time comes.

By Friday evening I had 47 acres prepared for planting pumpkins! Jeff Petterson helped me on Saturday Plant 21 acres of pumpkins over at Wayne's. Danielle Lahr called about 6:30 that evening telling me that she had almost made it to my house I had to talk her there the last mile I was at Wayne's longer than I should have been. Wayne had laid down and took a nap and didn't get my trailer lights done, so I was late getting home. After a good breakfast we started planting mini pumpkins and squash that day. I told Danielle that she was the first lady to ride and plant on the pumpkin planter by the end of the day we had the 14 acre field planted! I didn't want to tell Danielle that here face had turned green during the day from the seed treatment, but she found out when she went to wash up! During the course of conversation Danielle mentioned that she had been to Orr Mn camp the last year it was held there, and that she would like to go back there sometime to see the place where she was baptized.

I thought it interesting that afternoon when Tom Kennebeck called and said they were in the area moving his son Chris back to Orr! Tom was wondering if we could meet later in the evening for a meal in Mankato. Tom is the pastor of North land community church up in Orr and worked at the camp the summer Danielle was up there! I could really see God involved with that one! It was quite refreshing to have Danielle help me for a couple of Days I don't get to have the company of young lady's around here much, and quite a change from the guys I normally work with! Danielle planted seeds as well as any of the help I ever had! I got the opportunity to show Danielle all the ground in 3 counties that I farm so she had an idea of my operation. I let Danielle drive the tractor while I planted for a bit so she could tell her class that she got to drive a tractor by herself! She told me they all clapped for her when she told them about that! Danielle teaches music in Independence Wisconsin. She is also trying to get a coffee house going in Eau Claire with several others to help assist women who have been sold into the sex slave trade from Cambodia. I think I phrased that right! By 3 pm on Monday we had finished planting the 12 acre field that I had prepared for that day! I was sorry to see Danielle leave I got to know my sister in Christ a little better than I had! Also she makes the best scrambled eggs and fresh mushrooms I believe I have eaten. To a single man any time a woman cooks for you that means a lot! Thanks Danielle it was a great weekend and I am glad you came! This week I got another 12 acres planted in between rains 60 acres of pumpkins planted all total with 15 yet to go! Who knows when those last acres will get planted as we had heavy rains here again this weekend? Hay will be ready to cut first crop next weekend so summer is fast approaching! My Neighbor Ernie is getting ready to move he had me over for supper on Saturday

I couldn't do anything any way because of the rain! Ernie had invited a mutual friend someone I hadn't seen since High school! We had a lot to talk about mostly how the Lord was working in our lives now. After I left Ernie's I stopped to my next door neighbors as Krissa Scholtz was having a graduation party! I was asking Krissa what she planned on doing with her life, and that she was probably tired of hearing that line! She said she really didn't know just yet what she was going to do. I told Krissa that I didn't know what I was going to do yet when I grew up neither! Like usual that line gets a lot of laughs from young and old alike, trouble is I'm always serious! I feel some days I may be getting somewhat reclusive because I always have to force myself to go to these things. After I am there I enjoy being there. Us old farm boys always like to talk of how things used to be and how they are today! I figure it never hurt me to grow up the way I did! I wouldn't change anything about how my life has went good or bad. I am glad to be in the position of life I am now and although at times life can be hard it is still good to have lived! Someday Jesus will return!

Matthew 24:27-31

The Arrival of the Son of Man isn't something you go to see. He comes like swift lightning to you! **28** Whenever you see crowds gathering, think of carrion vultures circling, moving in, hovering over a rotting carcass. You can be quite sure that it's not the living Son of Man pulling in those crowds. **29** "Following those hard times, Sun will fade out, moon cloud over, Stars fall out of the sky, cosmic powers tremble. **30**"Then, the Arrival of the Son of Man! It will fill the skies–no one will miss it. Unready people all over the world, outsiders to the splendor and power, will raise a huge lament as they watch the Son of Man blazing out of heaven. **31** At that same moment, he'll dispatch his angels with a trumpet-blast summons, pulling in God's chosen from the four winds, from pole to pole.

And things will be different than they are now!
Blessings to you all!
In Christ
George Denn

# Hey by George! August 6-7 2014

# BUGS, MUD, AND HOPE!

Matthew 8-23-27

**23** Then he got in the boat, his disciples with him. **24** The next thing they knew, they were in a severe storm. Waves were crashing into the boat–and he was sound asleep! **25** They roused him, pleading, "Master, save us! We're going down!" **26** Jesus reprimanded them. "Why are you such cowards, such faint-hearts?" Then he stood up and told the wind to be silent, the sea to quiet down: "Silence!" The sea became smooth as glass. **27** The men rubbed their eyes, astonished. "What's going on here? Wind and sea come to heel at his command!

Sometime early in June I noticed them, little black and yellow critters despised by anyone who grows curcubits. Otherwise known as pumpkins squash and gourds! The cucumber beetle and I have had battles in the past, and in the past I just sprayed them and that was the end of them, however as an organic farmer now that is

172

not an option. On non organic land I use a treated seed a couple of chews on a plant and that is the end of them, but on organic land that is not an option ether! By the time they were done with me they had chewed up 21 acres of pumpkins and 6 acres of squash! These bugs can eat up a seedling in a day and most plants had 5-6 bugs on them far more than I had ever seen before! Any attempt to remove them would be very time consuming and costly, and since I had neither the time or the money, I knew I had to go to the only one that had wisdom for this situation, God!

> James 1: 4-7
> **4** So don't try to get out of anything prematurely. Let it do its work so you become mature and well-developed, not deficient in any way. **5** If you don't know what you're doing, pray to the Father. He loves to help. You'll get his help, and won't be condescended to when you ask for it. **6** Ask boldly, believingly, without a second thought. People who "worry their prayers" are like wind-whipped waves. **7** Don't think you're going to get anything from the Master that way.

I called my friend Jeff and told him we should pray for this situation, for wisdom what to do or a solution to this problem. We were already having a wet year here in Minnesota, but God sent us 5 inches of rain one night shortly after we prayed that did get rid of the bugs, but it bought all farm work in the most critical time of the year to a complete stand still for about 2 weeks! It is things like this that caused me to coin the phrase "be careful what you want you might get it!" For a man of the soil to sit around and do nothing for

2 weeks during the most critical time of the year when he should be working the very hardest he can, is like Asking a doctor to stop a surgery shortly after he had started! Or a teacher not to teach after class is in session. Or a policeman just to sit there and do nothing while crimes are being committed all around him. Anyhow I think you get the picture if not use your imagination I am sure you will come up with something! I had hay that we had just gotten baled before it rained and needed to be stored but the field was so wet after that all you did was mush down if you tried to go get it. I had this hay tested not long ago it came back "serious mold should not be feed to livestock" why did I even put that stuff in the shed and who needs $9000 dollars anyway? Excuse me for being somewhat sarcastic but I think this year has done something to me! There were pumpkins that need to be planted yet, and pumpkins that need to be replanted, and cultivating to be done, but all one could was wait! When I could start field work again everything need doing all at once! As I write this I am still trying to catch up on work, and it is practically mid-August already! If farm work can't be done in an orderly fashion it all becomes discombobulated! I don't know if that is an actual word I am sure if those who come up with words would try their hand at farming it would probably become one quickly! When I walked up to my tractor after letting it sit so long I noticed the tool box was missing, as well as its 2 battery's, I have been robbed! This led me to think where are you Jesus I thought you were protecting things? $260 dollars latter I was back in business! Day by day it was hard to remain positive with everything around being so negative, but at least the bugs were gone! God had drowned them in all that rain, so a prayer had been answered. The night crawlers had also drowned, and the land stunk! The soil was still muddy when I started to cultivate,

and it stuck to the shovels. I couldn't wait any longer as weeds were taking over! I had to destroy a field of Oats so I had a dry spot to plant pumpkins on. The field I intended to plant them on finally got planted on the 4th of July! I had to cultivate, and had to replant so I hooked up the planter in a make shift way to the cultivator. I put an anvil on the cultivator to displace the weight of the guy riding the planter. I am sure this was a sight to passersby, but it worked well and I saved a day doing it that way! I could look across the field and see the hay laying yet that I had cut earlier in the month drowned out and smothered by too much rain it had been too wet to get the hay off. Never since I had been working out in the fields since I was a boy had I seen a year like this! It was real hard to remain positive, surrounded by so much negativity! The few farmers I had talked with seemed to be relying on the fact that they had federal crop insurance. I don't have any; I always believed that God was my insurance policy. As I was cultivating one day looking at all the negativity I think I know how the disciples felt when they thought Jesus didn't seem to care if they drowned in that boat so long ago! I too felt that Jesus was asleep and didn't seem to care much about my situation. All of a sudden something within side of me seemed to be point out that I was going to let this situation keep me down, or I was going to stand up to it and look it in the eye so to speak! I was going to do what I could do and trust God for the rest. So on that tractor that day I asked God for the strength to move forward and stand up to it, because I had none left!

Psalm 29:1-11

**1** Bravo, God, bravo! Gods and all angels shout, "Encore!" **2** In awe before the glory, in awe before God's visible power. Stand at attention! Dress your

175

best to honor him! **3** God thunders across the waters, Brilliant, his voice and his face, streaming brightness–God, across the flood waters. **4** God's thunder tympanic, God's thunder symphonic. **5** God's thunder smashes cedars, God topples the northern cedars. **6** The mountain ranges skip like spring colts, The high ridges jump like wild kid goats. **7** God's thunder spits fire. **8** God thunders, the wilderness quakes; He makes the desert of Kadesh shake. **9** God's thunder sets the oak trees dancing A wild dance, whirling; the pelting rain strips their branches. We fall to our knees–we call out, "Glory!" **10** Above the floodwaters is God's throne from which his power flows, from which he rules the world. **11** God makes his people strong. God gives his people peace.

I personally feel most folks should have to grow their own food for at least one year of their life; it may give them a better perspective of what all goes into it before it reaches them! Northern light camp started the 5 of July I was only 2 days late I had to finish cultivating pumpkins before I could go. Thank God the hay still had some water standing in it so that could be left until I got back from camp! When I arrived at Northern light camp it sure was good to see everyone. I had to teach a noodle making class. I was lucky to be there so I had no time to prepare. Doug's wood working class put aside what they were working on, and turned me out a rolling pin, out of a piece of maple fire wood, on Doug's lathe. After my noodle making class I gave this to Jake and Alex the 2 guys that helped make it they took it home to San Diego California and gave it to their mom. I borrowed some utensils and kettle and cooking station from John who was teaching a canning session, and Troy went to town and got me the flour and eggs I needed! So I had seen how God had taken care of things even if I hadn't! Anthony Mullins was there, he is in charge of the many GCI camps evidently while I was taking a cat nap he took a picture of me and put it on face book. For some reason this humors many people. He also made the announcement that I would like to climb the rock wall this was unbeknown to me of course! That I wanted to climb the wall, but I was looking for a chance to challenge myself this year my chance had come! I figured I could make it to the top before the 2 lady's had my climbing harness on! And with the agility of superman, (well maybe not quite that agile) I climbed to the top and touched the ceiling! Cheers went up from the spectators below and when I came down they all told me to jump so I did! This picked Linda the person who was belaying right off the ground! Good thing she had a harness on and was chained to the floor, or she would have gone up to the top far faster than I did! I think we had 23 campers and as many staff. I went river canoeing twice, had 2 noodle making classes this year we had buttered noodles, yummy! There was a session for pioneer life I was the only one that didn't have to ware those silly suspenders they hand out as I already had on bib overalls! My character was a farmer's son and they had me working on the farm from morning till night, so even in a different life things are much the same as they had been in this one! I have great respect for those early people they had to work so hard to build this country, and they past that work ethic on to their sons and grandsons. Last fall I had a worker tell me that I was a tough person. This amused me, I told him if you think I am tough, you ought to have seen the people who raised me! Those people were tough, I don't even come

177

close! I wonder what those old people would think if they could come back today, it is probably a good thing that they can't! Going to Northern light camp was a great respite for me and I came home rejuvenated! I had exactly 12 days to get the rest of my work done before Heartland camp, and I was discouraged to see it raining the day I got back. The next day however I was able to start cutting hay the field had dried out while I was at camp. I had to cut half of my Oats crop for hay 33 acres it had rust in is so bad there was nothing in the heads. Rust is a fungus oats get in wet weather. I was raking these oats for baling thinking of all the work I had yet to do when Ethan Gibson drove up asking if I had anything he could do? Ethan had worked for me for many years some years back. I had a hay field over at Wayne's farm that had been destroyed by the flooding that needed plowing, disking, and planted to oats yet. I told Ethan if he wanted to do those things that would be great! I also told him that he was a grown man now and should be able to figure things out without my help. God had sent Ethan that day or I never would have gotten those things accomplished! I got the hay all put up, pumpkins got all cultivated, oats planted, the rest of my crop of Oats I hired a guy to swath for combining, and arranged for the oats to be combined while I was gone to Heartland camp! Whew! Now I could leave without thinking of things back here! Someone even paid me for some hay the day before I went so I had funds to go on, and it was raining here the day I left for camp! This was to be my 11 th year serving at heartland camp. As I was doing my duties, driving people to and fro, and hauling water to various activity sites. I couldn't help but notice the old archery site all grown up to weeds! It also was much smaller than the site they are using now! The old paintball site where many a battle had taken place is now head high with grass and weeds you can barely see some of the things we used to hide behind and the old shed is almost ready to fall down! It was abandoned last year because of the flooding that took place, and moved to the woods. So we don't have to haul people way down there anymore, so I don't have near so much to do! I don't like the course where it is now, I belong to the times of the one down below where many friendships were formed and much fun was had! Looking at the weeds and the over grown course it gave me an Erie felling! Wondering if our time in those places had been in vain? I had to tell myself no!

Hebrews 13:8

**8** For Jesus doesn't change–yesterday, today, tomorrow, he's always totally himself.

Even though my mind wants to look at past things with fondness, they are gone, and I must force myself to live in today's world instead of the past! Solomon also wrote something concerning this.

Ecclesiastes 7:10

**10** Don't always be asking, "Where are the good old days?" Wise folks don't ask questions like that.

One of the strangest things to happen this year at camp to me was this. One morning I had went to the office when I was getting back on the gator the clip for my 2 way radio had vanished I couldn't find it anywhere. I drove down to chapel and took part in the worship service. When they started to sing the last song I went to the rest room. When I returned I was standing there for some reason I looked under the seat that was to my right, and there was the radio clip for number

16 my radio! Strange! It was good to spend the week working with friends; in the end about 7 were baptized. Again Camp was like a respite for me! After camp gets over, and everyone starts to leave, to me this is a very sad time, and I always seem to get emotional to everyone that I say goodbye to! Who knows if some of them I will ever see again on this side of things. A lot can go on in a year's time, and who knows when any of us will depart from this life! This reality gets more apparent as one gets older! The crops looked good until we got back to Minnesota! Everything is now bone dry the oats that were harvested while I was gone were put into a bin nobody wants them at this time. They only ran 40 bushel to the acre less than half of what they should have! The $20,000 dollar hay deal I had been working on since mid-camp week became a mirage as well! I just hate mirages! The guy found someone out in North Dakota that would truck it to him cheaper! The funds that I came home with from camp went fast, for parts, and gas! I look at all these things and have to wonder Jesus where are you in all of this? I have to remind myself that I have witnessed more miracles with an empty billfold than I ever did a full one! I came across this scripture in my daily devotional on my way home from camp.

Lamentations 3:16-24

He ground my face into the gravel. He pounded me into the mud. **17** I gave up on life altogether. I've forgotten what the good life is like. **18** I said to myself, "This is it. I'm finished. God is a lost cause." It's a Good Thing to Hope for Help from God **19** I'll never forget the trouble, the utter lostness, the taste of ashes, the poison I've swallowed. **20** I remember it all–oh, how well I remember–the feeling of hitting the bottom. **21** But there's one other thing I remember, and remembering, I keep a grip on hope: **22** God's loyal love couldn't have run out, his merciful love couldn't have dried up. **23** They're created new every morning. How great your faithfulness! **24**I'm sticking with God (I say it over and over). He's all I've got left.

Although at times it can be hard to believe I must force myself to believe this is true and it will be very interesting to see how this year ends up!

Gods' peace and blessings to you all!

In Christ

George Denn

# Hey By George! November 8-24 2014

# A DIFFERENT HARVEST TIME!

John 15:1-2

**"I** am the Real Vine and my Father is the Farmer. **2** He cuts off every branch of me that doesn't bear grapes. And every branch that is grape-bearing he prunes back so it will bear even more.

As I start to write this story I am in Germantown Illinois, staying at the home of David and Shirley Worsfold. I am down in this neck of the woods because Blue needed a ride back to Peoria. Blue is a Black man that I met at summer camp a couple years ago, God sent him up to work for me last fall in the pumpkins, via a fellow friend David Salanders. You will Meet Blue later on in my story for I must back up until August for any of this to make any sense! Every year seems to be far different than the one that has preceded it. This year I had been praying for quality help, after the disastrous year I had last year with help! I was sort of dreading fall to come again, and it is my favorite season! Ely Vogel was the first one to show up this year. Ely had been working for neighbor David, and helped me with the straw baling this year. Ely had been between jobs so he needed the work. One of the things that I really appreciated about Ely was that he had grown up on a farm and he was well familiar with stacking bales so I didn't have to teach him a thing! In less than a week Ely and I got the straw all baled and put in a shed out of the weather. The guy that was supposed to be helping with this was Josh, but he ran out of gas literally! I had been calling him for 4 days when I got back from camp, but was unable to get a hold of him. Finally on the last day of stacking straw, Josh called. I told Josh to come to where we were working but he told me he didn't have enough gas to get there! I told him where he could find some but Josh never came. When I got home that day my old pickup was sitting in the yard, Josh had cleaned out his stuff and went home, he had quit before I could fire him! After the straw was done I told Ely that if he still needed work this fall he was welcome to come help harvest the pumpkin crop. Ely did return and in between family commitments was a great worker! The next person to show up was a young man from Italy his name in English is Joseph Crow. I told Joseph that he was in America now and needed an American name so I told him I was going to call him Joe Crow! Joe Crow is a friend of my former hired man Joe Kruse who is now a monk in Italy. Joe Crow stayed at Joe Kruse's aunt and uncle's farm right across the road from me. Joe was here in America to experience farm life for 3 months. Often when he was able Joe would come and help us with the pumpkin harvest. Before that a couple times he helped me load hay. Several times I told him he was carrying the bales way to hi in the air with the skid loader he found out one day what I meant by that, and why one wears seat belts when he is in a skid loader. If not for that belt he would have went flying through the air it still amuses me to remember it! I firmly believe experience is the best teacher, because once something like that happens to you, believe me you never forget it! Joe Crow helped me get a couple of my stands set up.

I also showed Joe Crow how to drive my tractor and let him drive my pickup when we were away from main roads! One day we were out driving down the road when a cop stopped me for not wearing seat belts. I said a prayer under my breath and the cop let us go with just a warning! After that every time we drove somewhere Joe Crow would remind me, "ok Mr. George it is seat belt time!" One day we were driving by the county jail I told Joe Crow that's where they put you if you can't behave yourself! He seemed quite amused by that! Joe Crow helped me put up most of my stands. One place had standing corn where I put my stand. I sawed the corn down with my chain saw and showed Joe how to tie it into bundles. Joe Crow never saw any one ever harvest corn this way. I told Joe that all he had to remember about me was that I was a savage and that would help him to make sense of some of the things that I do! Later one day I took him with me when I cut corn with my corn binder; it is way faster than cutting and tying by hand! Again Joe Crow was fascinated by what he saw he made this statement that the ancient machine is quite faster than the modern machine for this job! I told him that was the way it was in my world! I had to say goodbye to my Italian friend on November 1, as he was going back home the following Monday. He thought it funny that I indeed got stopped buy the cops again, and this time I was issued a ticket for not wearing my seatbelts! After I left the neighbors that night Joe Crow stuck his head out the door and made this statement. "It is seat belt time Mr. Denn!"

Ashley Block called and wondered when she should come to work. It would be the 3 year Ashley would work for me! This year Ely wanted to be paid in change so he could go through it to see if he could find any valuable coins. So I had to tell Ashley that I had to pay her in silver bars this year. The silver bars that I gave her for her pay were $1 bills rapped in tin foil! Ashley told Jeff that this was her dream Job, and that she wanted to do this for the next 40 years! I bought this old 93 ford Half ton pickup for hauling pumpkins. Its previous owner was bragging it up how good it was. The young guys name was Otto he seemed to grimace when I told him what I was going to use it for, and I said it only has to last 2 months as far as I was concerned! When I got home I couldn't get it started, I felt I had been taken in by a collage kid! I figured it out, I named it curse 2 and I gave it to Ashley for her bonus at the end of the season. I told her if she wants to work for me next year she needs to learn how to drive a 5 speed, and if she is successful, I will buy it back from her next season if it was still running, or she could sell it for scrap and get about $400. It was up to her what she wants to do!

Booker T. Blakes or Blue as he is called is a black man I met a few years ago at summer camp I could probably write a whole book about this guy, but I will try to contain myself! Blue is a character so that makes him a man after my own heart! Last summer while I was at camp Blue was dropping off some youth; he was telling me that he wanted to come up to my place during pumpkin time. I was telling Blue that would be fine as that time of year I generally need all the help I can get! Blue showed up on September 9 after several failed attempts at getting a bus ride. David Slanders personally drove Blue the 7 hours here and then drove back to Peoria that very night! Blue is 64 years old and resides at Heavens View church in Peoria Illinois. Blue is the only person that I know of to be shot twice he can show you the bullet wounds at any time his story really impressed everyone here! One day Jesus got a hold of Blue and he threw his guns into the river, instead of killing the people he intended too, he went to church with Pastor Tony Pierce and his wife instead! Every time Blue told his story people were fascinated! He even had a big impact on David Maki the guy who stays here. That impressed me more than anything! Blue was telling me one day that his grandpa used to farm with mules down in Mississippi. He was telling me that when the mules thought it was time to quit for the day they would just lay down and refuse to work anymore! Blues grandpa said if he took some dry grass and kindling wood and put that under the mule's belly, and light that on fire the mule would get up and practically drag his grandpa across the field! One morning after that Blue was saying "George I'm feeling like I didn't want to work today!" I told Blue I'd have to get some dry grass and kindling wood! What time did you say we were to be ready for work" Blue said! Blues favorite saying is" what we have here is a failure to communicate, I've got to get your mind right!" Blue and Ashley were pretty much a team Blue called her Miss Ashley! I swear if somebody would be here in the fall with a movie camera there would be a fortune to be made!

My friend Jeff helped again in between being pastor for Madelia Church of Christ and his Dental drug running job. Jeff pretty much takes care of the stand over there 40 miles from here on Sundays he would take Blue to church with him so he would have help afterward to stock the stand.

One day not much before the season started my friend Bob Spiegler asked me to lunch at the Bonfire. In the course of conversation he asked me if I had enough help for the fall harvest. "Not really" was my answer I was just waiting on God to supply the workers. Bob was mentioning that he had just met a person that was a head of the R.O.T.C. program here at the collage in Mankato though fellowship of Christian Athletes. Bobs friend Dennis Murphy called me that afternoon he was telling me his recruits were looking for something like this for a fund raiser in the end more than 15 people volunteered for operation pick pumpkin! R.O.T.C. or Reserve officer training corps showed me that God will even send you the U.S. army if he has too, in order to answer a prayer! Cadet Bryce Hickman was the man in charge of the troops I believe Bryce is 22 I told Bryce that he could refer to me as General George if he wanted too! Sept 13 was there first mission things were not ripening as they should this year and I was dragging my feet when normally we would be running. I sent them to my weediest field to put into rows ripe pumpkins. They found very few ripe ones and it turned into jungle war fair with the weeds many got discouraged including myself when I and my workers saw how they had picked! In my friend Blues words, " what we have here is a failure to communicate, I've got to get their minds right! The next Saturday only Bryce and a girl showed up and they said they could only stay until 1 PM! We did get the pie pumpkins picked that morning that I had intended for that day so mission accomplished! The next weekend they couldn't come because they had a training weekend. And the next Saturday the group picked large pumpkins things were looking up! Bryce couldn't be there the next weekend so he put Cadet Roman in charge of the group. I was un sure if Roman was the right person for the Job but I was wrong! Roman led his crew without a fault and we picked all the large squash and pie pumpkins that day! One thing I remember about Roman was he didn't like his name. I never cared for mine when I was a young person but have since come to appreciate it. I hope Roman will grow to appreciate his name as well someday! The final weekend the R.O.T.C. people were here we did a reconnaissance mission on some pie pumpkins Bryce seemed to be impressed that I knew that the word reconnaissance came from the word reconnoiter which means to look over the land for military purpose! In my old family catholic bible which was the first version I ever read Numbers 13:1-2 reads as follows.

Numbers 13: 1-2

1 The Lord said to Moses, 2 "Send men to reconnoiter the land of Canaan, which I am giving to the Israelites. You shall send one man from each ancestral tribe, all of them princes."

By this act I was able to get another load of pie pumpkins and we finished the day picking the last of the large pumpkins on Wayne Schwartz's farm. When the day was finished I was able to give Bryce and Roman a copy of my books and explain to them that this was the ministry God put me in charge of," the ministry of Joy!"

With only 61 days to make the bulk of my income I have very few days that I won't pick. One morning it was raining, so naturally Blue thought we wouldn't be picking that day! To Blues surprise I showed him how we could take a 30 gallon garbage sack and poke a hole for your head and 2 for your arms so we could indeed pick in the rain! Joe Crow was there that day to help as we were picking the rain was falling harder and one of the pickups couldn't climb the hill so we had to abandon it. That meant 4 had to ride home in one pickup so 2 of us had to ride in back. I told Ashley to drive and Blue to get up front also, me and Joe Crow got to ride the 3 miles back home in the rain! Joe Crow told me it was the coldest he had ever been! Joe Crow called out to Jesus to forgive his sins. I assured Joe Crow that Jesus already had!

Romans 5:12-20

**12** You know the story of how Adam landed us in the dilemma we're in–first sin, then death, and no one exempt from either sin or death. **13** That sin disturbed relations with God in everything and everyone, but the extent of the disturbance was not clear until God spelled it out in detail to Moses. So death, this huge abyss separating us from God, dominated the landscape from Adam to Moses. **14** Even those who didn't sin precisely as Adam did by disobeying a specific command of God still had to experience this termination of life, this separation from God. But Adam, who got us into this, also points ahead to the One who will get us out of it. **15** Yet the rescuing gift is not exactly parallel to the death-dealing sin. If one man's sin put crowds of people at the dead-end abyss of separation from God, just think what God's gift poured through one man, Jesus Christ, will do! **16** There's no comparison between that death-dealing sin and this generous, life-giving gift. The verdict on that one sin was the death sentence; the verdict on the many sins that followed was this wonderful life sentence. **17** If death got the upper hand through one man's wrongdoing, can you imagine the breathtaking recovery life makes, sovereign life, in those who grasp with both hands this wildly extravagant life-gift, this grand setting-everything-right, that the one man Jesus Christ provides? **18** Here it is in a nutshell: Just as one person did it wrong and got us in all this trouble with sin and death, another person did it right and got us out of it. But more than just getting us out of trouble, he got us into life! **19** One man said no to God and put many people in the wrong; one man said yes to God and put many in the right. **20** All that passing laws against sin did was produce more lawbreakers. But sin didn't, and doesn't, have a chance in competition with the aggressive forgiveness we call grace. When it's sin versus grace, grace wins hands down.

It had been a long time since I had been that cold and wet myself. We all dried of changed cloths ate some lunch. Ready or not we headed over to Wayne Schwartz's that afternoon to pick large pumpkins. I needed to have a minimum of 4 loads for the next day. One of the pickups over heated by the abuse we inflicted on it that day in the mud! We were down to our last load when Wayne called and asked if we were picking in this weather I told him we were he said he had the wood stove going and hot coffee for all. I told Wayne I would mention it to my crew. I did, but also told them to forget it if we go in their now we would never come out! What most people don't realize is that if we don't get this stuff picked, and keep ahead of people buying it, we get behind. If that happens to you, you never catch up! I say this from experience. In the end I told my crew I was proud of them not one quit and not one complained we all just did what needed to be done! It was through this experience that God spoke to me. Nobody realizes what it takes to get these pumpkins and squash to them for others to experience Joy. Nobody realizes not in its magnitude what Jesus went through to give us eternal life, we really have no idea!

Sunday October 12 was a pumpkin picking fundraiser day for various youth camps in my churches region. I was in the lead pickup heading to a pumpkin field. 2 youth were in the pickup with me Sterling and Hunter. We were on this gravel road and had to cross state hwy 60. I stopped at the stop sign looked both ways saw nothing and proceeded across the hwy. Before I could get across the highway a car came out of nowhere half on the road and half in the ditch probably going the speed limit passing perpendicular just feet in front of us! "What just happened?" Hunter exclaimed. "We damn near got killed!" was my answer. God must have a purpose for one of you guys lives! What was weird about that indecent was I had been thinking of a scenario like that all morning!

Psalm 139:1-10

**1** God, investigate my life; get all the facts firsthand. **2** I'm an open book to you; even from a distance, you know what I'm thinking. **3** You know when I leave and when I get back; I'm never out of your sight. **4** You know everything I'm going to say before I start the first sentence. **5** I look behind me and you're there, then up ahead and you're there, too–your reassuring presence, coming and going. **6** This is too much, too wonderful–I can't take it all in! **7** Is there anyplace I can go to avoid your Spirit? to be out of your sight? **8** If I climb to the sky, you're there! If I go underground, you're there! **9** If I flew on morning's wings to the far western horizon, **10** You'd find me in a minute–you're already there waiting!

I could defiantly see the hand of God protecting us that day. If he hadn't been I wouldn't be writing this right now! On Monday October 20 we only had 6 more acres of large pumpkins to pick I was figuring that the way the rest of them yielded there should be about 24 loads left to pick. By noon however we had picked all that were any good 6 loads! These pumpkins were the ones I had planted on July 4th. They were poor at best! Frost had damaged a lot of the better looking ones! They were just not ripe enough when the frost had hit, so they decayed! I had no choice but to inform my crew that this would be the last day of regular work! I was just as surprised as they were! That afternoon was spent filling my basement and porch with fire wood for the coming winter 6 loads in all a little more than 1/3 of what it takes to heat this place! Like I told my neighbor Fred once, it takes a lot of wood to heat a corn crib!

Ely Vogel was the first person to be let go, but neighbor David needed his help again so Ely went back over their instead of coming here. I hated to see Ely Go he was such a good worker, but I had no more work for him, so that's the way it is. We all prayed for Ely that God would give him a job that would sustain his family. Last I heard after he was done at David's, Jack Links hired him to make beef jerky!

Lynne Pahl and grandson Nick came that Thursday to help pick pumpkins I had left some pie pumpkins to pick for that day. After that Nick, Lynne, and Blue helped me haul some hay in that was still out in the field. One of the days they helped, I loaded Blues load full of round bales and told him to take it back to the yard. I was loading Nicks load when I noticed Blue driving all over the field to and fro with his load of hay! Here he was lost! So Lynne walked over to him and pointed the way he should go! This all was amusing to me but

Blue is from inner city Peoria, and not acquainted with farm terms and ways, and I am sure if I had to try and find my way their I would have my troubles as well!

61 days comes and go's mighty fast! In that time I don't sleep a whole lot. Usually I am up around 4 am there is always something to be done. Popcorn to put in jars, a load of straw to be taken to a stand or some other business to be taken care of before my workers get here at 8 am. I never imagined that I would be the boss of anyone so I want to be the best one I can be. To me that means working side by side with them and never asking them to do anything that I wouldn't do myself. An average day will find me picking pumpkins and filling trucks or emptying them at the 6 various stands that have become so familiar in southern Minnesota. I try to be finish with the workers around 5 but my day isn't over until the money from the stands is collected, counted and documented generally this is about 9 o'clock in the evening, my friend Jeff usually is the one to help me with the collecting and counting process. This year with the lack of product I decided to take a couple of smaller stands down a few days early. This would keep the larger ones stocked until the very end. I had no idea if this was the right thing to do as I never had to do it before! There was no more to do with the pumpkins until it was time to take the rest of the stands down, so I was able to get my fall plowing done before I took the rest of the stands down, after the first weekend in November. As I was plowing there seemed to be a spirit of peace settle over the land. The struggles that had led up to this year's harvest were history so was the wonderment of how the crop would turn out! It is in this time I can actually think and consider the year that had just passed! For some years now I could see that growing and harvesting hay has been in conflict with my

pumpkin business. Producing hay was always a way to make money for me, and raising pumpkins was always something I had devoted to God. Never knowing what the outcome or how much income I would make on them! I could see this scripture becoming very real in my life!

Matthew 6:24

**24** "You can't worship two gods at once. Loving one god, you'll end up hating the other. Adoration of one feeds contempt for the other. You can't worship God and Money both

All year I was despising the time I spent with the hay and loved the time I spent with the pumpkins so I will listen to the prompting of the Holy Spirit in this area of my life and discontinue Hay, except for a small amount for the pumpkin stands. I see no future in the hay business and it would be foolish on my part to continue it.

Proverbs 22:3

**3** A prudent person sees trouble coming and ducks; a simpleton walks in blindly and is clobbered.

So after this year I will have 144 acres less hay to harvest that ground has been rented to others! And after the hay I have on hand is sold there will be no more "Hay by George!" It was the Lord that gave me that business and now he has taken it away!

Job 1:21

**21**Naked I came from my mother's womb, naked I'll
return to the womb of the earth. God gives, God takes.
God's name be ever blessed.

As we were taking the stands down Blue mentioned that there
seems to be a sadness to it all at the end of the season. I have experienced this "sadness" for years, so I know what he was talking about!
One day not long ago my friend Jeff and I were talking about this
and Jeff offered his opinion. All fall you experience seeing the joy
in people it is part of the fall harvest, you don't experience this kind
of joy any other harvest, but the fall one. He is right summer harvest
of small grain it is usually hot and miserable! So when the fall harvest is over you experience sadness it is the opposite of joy. Could
all be? Sunday Nov 9th I had to say goodbye to my friend Blue it
was no easy thing! Later that afternoon another friend Steve Gebrin
took me on a tour of the area! He took me to see where all the beer
barons once lived! I noticed some of those places had 4 chimneys
coming out of the roofs! These were built when coal or wood was
the only heat source. I told Steve I was glad not to have to cut the
wood for those places! Steve was taking me to see the Libby's fac-
tory in Morton Illinois were they can all the pumpkins. As he drove
Steve was telling a story from way back when some of his ances-
tors were hauling a piano on a horse drawn wagon they didn't tie
it down and the piano rolled and crashed out of the wagon down a
steep embankment and smashed to smithereens! The way I imagine
that is way too humorous! After we saw the canning co., at the last
moment Steve said there is as pumpkin farm just down this road I'll
show you. We meet the owner John Acherman. I found out in the

course of conversation that John was a Christian we were both the same age, and that he has been raising pumpkins about as long as I have! John knows all too well about the spirit of "sadness" when the year is over!

Now that I am back in Minnesota and as I look over the snowy landscape while finishing this story I can finally bring closer to the year that is behind. Some of the things I tried worked and some did not! I am glad I prevailed through it, but really it was Jesus helping me all the way! I have to laugh as I start to think about ordering seeds for next year something that I started all of 15 years ago to supplement my income will from this point on will be my income! In this I have no fears. Actually I'm looking forward to it! I close this story with this thought.

Psalm 145

**1** I lift you high in praise, my God, O my King! and I'll bless your name into eternity. **2** I'll bless you every day, and keep it up from now to eternity. **3** God is magnificent; he can never be praised enough. There are no boundaries to his greatness. **4** Generation after generation stands in awe of your work; each one tells stories of your mighty acts. **5** Your beauty and splendor have everyone talking; I compose songs on your wonders. **6** Your marvelous doings are head-line news; I could write a book full of the details of your greatness. **7** The fame of your goodness spreads across the country; your righteousness is on every-one's lips. **8** God is all mercy and grace–not quick to anger, is rich in love. **9** God is good to one and all; everything he does is suffused with grace. **10** Creation and creatures applaud you, God; **11** your holy people bless you. They talk about the glories of your rule, they exclaim over your splendor, **12** Letting the world know of your power for good, the lavish splendor of your kingdom. **13** Your kingdom is a kingdom eternal; you never get voted out of office. God always does what he says, and is gracious in everything he does. **14** God gives a hand to those down on their luck, gives a fresh start to those ready to quit.**15** All eyes are on you, expectant; you give them their meals on time. **16** Generous to a fault, you lavish your favor on all creatures. **17** Everything God does is right–the trademark on all his works is love. **18** God's there, listening for all who pray, for all who pray and mean it. **19** He does what's best for those who fear him–hears them call out, and saves them. **20** God sticks by all who love him, but it's all over for those who don't. **21** My mouth is filled with God's praise. Let everything living bless him, bless his holy name from now to eternity!

The end of one thing is always the beginning of something new!
In Christ,
George Denn

# TRIALS, TRIBULATION, AND ENCOURAGEMENT

1 Thessalonians 2:17-3:5

[17-20] Do you have any idea how very homesick we became for you, dear friends? Even though it hadn't been that long and it was only our bodies that were separated from you, not our hearts, we tried our very best to get back to see you. You can't imagine how much we missed you! I, Paul, tried over and over to get back, but Satan stymied us each time. Who do you think we're going to be proud of when our Master Jesus appears if it's not you? You're our pride and tearing down everything we had built up together.

3 [1-2] So when we couldn't stand being separated from you any longer and could find no way to visit you our- selves, we stayed in Athens and sent Timothy to get you up and about, cheering you on so you wouldn't be discouraged by these hard times. He's a brother and

companion in the faith, God's man in spreading the Message, preaching Christ.

3-5 Not that the troubles should come as any surprise to you. You've always known that we're in for this kind of thing. It's part of our calling. When we were with you, we made it quite clear that there was trouble ahead. And now that it's happened, you know what it's like. That's why I couldn't quit worrying; I had to know for myself how you were doing in the faith. I didn't want the Tempter getting to you and tearing down everything we had built up together.

I think I have entered a mid-life crisis, or am losing my mind. Possibly both! I just turned 53 this spring I have been feeling down for quite some time and my circumstances have me wondering and questioning pretty much everything. I entered winter with approximately $60,000 worth of hay to sell. This would propel me into the best financial shape I had ever been in, or so I thought! But alas at the time of this writing I still have $50,000 worth of hay to sell and pasture time is at hand and new crop hay will start to come of the fields in about 3 weeks. I guess that's what I get for not listening to the Holy Spirit about discontinuing this hay business sooner; he has been working on me for the last 3 years! God has finally gotten his point across by allowing 144 acres of land that I used to make hay on to be taken away. He has also allowed me to be embroiled in a law suit in where $21,000 worth of turkey manure was accidentally spread on my hayfield so according to some folks this has left me unjustly enriched! This of course my dear friend is a bunch of you know what! Because I could tell you exactly how enriched I have been! But today my message is more spiritual in nature.

Job 33:14-19
God always answers, one way or another,
    even when people don't recognize his presence.
15-18 "In a dream, for instance, a vision at night,
      when men and women are deep in sleep,
         fast asleep in their beds—
God opens their ears
      and impresses them with warnings
To turn them back from something bad they're planning,
      from some reckless choice,
And keep them from an early grave,
      from the river of no return.
19-22 "Or, God might get their attention through pain,
      by throwing them on a bed of suffering,

is God speaking to you my friends? Because just like Elihu tells Job the warnings do get more severe! After some prayers with some folks a few years back at snow blast, this scripture was brought to my attention by my pastor friend Richard Siedsclag.

1Samuel 3:1-10
[1-3] as at a time when the revelation of God was rarely heard or seen. One night Eli was sound asleep (his eyesight was very bad—he could hardly see). It was well before dawn; the sanctuary lamp was still burning. Samuel

was still in bed in the Temple of God, where the Chest
of God rested.

4-5 Then God called out, "Samuel, Samuel!"

Samuel answered, "Yes? I'm here." Then he ran to Eli saying, "I
heard you call. Here I am."
Eli said, "I didn't call you. Go back to bed." And so he did.

6-7 God called again, "Samuel, Samuel!"

Samuel got up and went to Eli, "I heard you call. Here I am."
Again Eli said, "Son, I didn't call you. Go back to bed." (This all
happened before Samuel knew God for himself. It was before the
revelation of God had been given to him personally.)

8-9 God called again, "Samuel!"—the third time! Yet
again Samuel got up and went to Eli, "Yes? I heard
you call me. Here I am."

That's when it dawned on Eli that God was calling the boy. So Eli
directed Samuel, "Go back and lie down. If the voice calls again, say,
'Speak, God. I'm your servant, ready to listen.'" Samuel returned
to his bed.

10 Then God came and stood before him exactly as
before, calling out, "Samuel! Samuel!"

Samuel answered, "Speak. I'm your servant, ready to listen."

I wasn't sure what God was trying to get across to me then, but I do now! Discontinue the hay business or suffer the consequences. I just hope I'm not to late. If I would have continued on another year it would have been.

Proverbs 27:12
A prudent person sees trouble coming and ducks; a simpleton walks in blindly and is clobbered.

It seems he is allowing some to sell just enough to keep things moving forward here. It sure turned out to be a depressing winter here. My seasonal depression was about as bad as it has ever been, and about all I did was sit around and keep wood in the stoves. Once in a while I go out to eat with three older guys I know. Bob is 65 still working for F.C.A David is 75 and is suffering from Alzheimer's. Jim is 91 a WW 2 vet they are always trying to get me the senior discount, but I tell them I'm not ready for that yet! Jim is a fascinating person to visit with, he can remember when he was young he knew several men who served in the civil war. One time he was in France for two weeks during wartime cold and starving they shot anything that moved! I asked Jim one day what's a 91 year old say when he gets up in the morning. What's there to eat was his answer! I was also able to take in a few outings like snow blast in January to western MN, and converge in March out in Ohio. It was nice to visit with friends at both places. I remember telling some folks about my hay not selling, that got back to the Peoria Church some were praying for my situation there.

Another situation that had been working on me for some time was David the guy who has lived here for the past 5 years. When David first came here this was a sanctuary for him, but after 5 years it has occurred to me that I have become an enabler! This is no small thing when the Lord points it out to you. Like all of us David has some issues and God wants to work on him just not here! So allowing David to stay any longer was not an option. I had it in mind to tell him he had to move on the 1st of April. I had to use tact, something I am short on. I hate confrontation and usually it ends up in an episode. I started to plant Oats that week so I was busy, David seemed to just disappear. Later I found out he was in the hospital with influenza and apparently his kidneys had shut down and was just a day from death! I hate to say it but it was sure nice around here to have the place to myself! On good Friday I was planting Oats I had my Dad stop and bring me something for dinner. After a while he drove out in the field where I was planting. Dad asked me how it was going. Alright I said, but sometimes I really wonder what I'm doing out here anymore! He laughed then he said I'm sorry George I should have let you go and work in town when you wanted to. What he was referring to was when I was 16 a friend of mine could get me a Job in town if I wanted. I told Dad this he kind of just hung his head and kicked at the ground.

I knew he needed my help so I sealed my fate that day and decided I would be a Farmer regardless of the cost! I told dad No, that I never regretted staying on the farm not one moment! Even if there never was a whole lot of money to be made, there is a freedom here that very few can say they have, and you can't put a price on that! That was just a 16 year old kid thinking his friend had something more glamorous than I had at the time! So no regrets! All too soon our visit was over, I worked side by side with dad many years until he had to stop helping me and take care of mother, it was like someone cut off my right arm! That night David returned from the hospital. I wanted to watch the Passion of the Christ. It's hard to watch The Passion of the Christ and tell a person who just got out of the hospital that he has to leave. My procrastinating nature told me to just hold off until after Easter. Monday came and went, David went to work that evening and I still hadn't brought it up. I went to bed that night knowing I had to deal with this issue! So I got back up and wrote David a note and stuck it in his bible so he couldn't miss it. He didn't read it for 2 days, when he did, he thanked me for the years I had let him stay here. David will be leaving here when he goes to his son Sam's graduation sometime the end of May. It will be nice to have the place to myself again! Sometime in mid-April I had to call David Worsfold to see if I could spend the night of the 19 at his place. During the course of conversation he asked me if my hay had sold. I told him it hadn't. David asked if I needed to borrow some money for springtime. Yes I needed to pay the rest of my spring land rent $5000. David told me to call a ascertain brother in the Lord who wanted to help me with my situation. I called this brother and he and another brother borrowed me 5000 dollars no interest and no questions asked to be paid back this fall at pumpkin time! The other day I stopped to talk with a neighbor who was out working in his field. He mentioned that he had to borrow money from a bank this year and was required to hand over his car titles, as well as sign over his machinery to the bank in case he couldn't pay back the loan. I realized while I was talking with this neighbor how fortunate I was to have met all the brothers and sisters I know while working at the youth camps! The scope of it goes way beyond what takes place at the camps! Even when a person is going through a trial it is better to be living in God's kingdom than out in the world! While at heartland camp training I asked for prayers for the hay. David Holmes suggested we pray about the turkey manure litigation as well. I can scarcely bring to words what it feels like to have so many brothers and sisters praying for you at one time! I was so close to Peoria that I went there to church the next day. My main reason was to visit with Blue but it is nice to see others as well! Blue mentioned that he couldn't go and eat with us that day; he had to get back and take care of his sister who had cancer. Blue called me this morning around 6 am he mentioned that his sister had passed on last week; I told Blue I was sorry to hear the news, but he assured me she was in a better place! I had lunch that day with Steve Geberin and Rose Vincent or "Mama Rose" as Blue calls her. After that my phone rang a guy from New Ulm Minnesota was looking for some hay, he bought $1000 worth of hay when I got home and I was encouraged, but went to my mail box and had a $600 bill from my Attorney and was discouraged! I remembered at this time a joke someone told of attorneys " Have you heard they bury Attorneys 10 feet deep when they die, They found out that really deep down they are good guys! It was good to spend the evening at David and Shirley Worsfolds. The next day the 20th was my 53 birthday after breakfast with David and Shirley I headed to Cousin Nancy's to pick up dad. We would head back to Minnesota the next morning. The next morning we did indeed head for home, dad's cousin Donna decided to come back with us. Then something very strange happened! We always take route 17 from Momence to Kankakee. That morning not too far out of Momence police had hwy 17 barricaded. We turned right down some country road always staying to the right of 17. We came upon a line of semi-trucks that had been detoured and were trying to get onto 17 but police had barricaded the road so they couldn't get on. Zigzagging down country roads we finally came to a place we could get back on 17. But when we came up to 17 we were on the opposite side and had to turn left to get onto it! The cops still had the road barricaded going the other direction. I told Dad and Donna that it was impossible for that to just have happened! Donna said I know. I know it was impossible to have crossed road 17 without having knowing it, and they had it barricaded at every point until where we got back on and there isn't a place where any road goes over or under it on that stretch of road! Later that day when we were almost home Nancy called us and told us someone had gotten killed on that road 17 around 5 am that morning! It is times like these that really make me question my sanity! They say that a person that is insane never questions their sanity so that must mean I'm alright I think?

Isaiah 55:8-9
"I don't think the way you think.
The way you work isn't the way I work."
GOD's Decree.
"For as the sky soars high above earth,
so the way I work surpasses the way you work,
and the way I think is beyond the way you think.

So who knows what that's all about! We have had such a nice spring this year compared to the last 2 that I have got all my work done until pumpkin planting time in mid to late May. I was able to help John Kruse (John is my former hired man Joe's brother) plow up some of his yard 2.5 acres so he can grow more garden crops this year. John lives 45 miles from me. On my way home one day I noticed all the large farmers planting their fields. I noticed this year most of them are using GPS to guide their machines across the fields the farmer is merely in the tractor to raise and lower the implement at the end of the field! This caused me to consider why do some people have so much while others have so little? I asked my 91 year old friend if he ever thought of such things. He said he had, then that makes one wonder if his life has any meaning! I have felt that very way a lot over the past 6 months! I wonder if that hay will ever sell perhaps David Holmes is right maybe I am too focused on the $50,000 value once and a while a little does sell! I only have to get through 3 more months and selling hay will no longer be an issue in my life! I was telling Wayne my landlord the other day, that it was a good thing I lost the first crop of hay on his place last year, or I would have that to sell as well. I also think of the statement Ann Kruse made last summer she mentioned the hay looked just beautiful and I was getting it put up with no rain, I mentioned to Ann that day that just because that was so It didn't mean a dang thing! I was right. It is sometimes hard to look at my brothers and sisters who work in town. Every week they go to work and every week they get paid for what they do, that is not always how it works out here! I also know that this is where God put me and I would be un happy in a lifestyle like that, I have been my own boss for too long! Even though I am in a down time of life, I can't seem to focus on anything spiritual, and question everything that is physical; I can still see Jesus at work around me. Just last Sunday my great nephew Josh who is 18 got baptized. He is excited to follow Jesus and after graduation will continue his schooling to become a pastor. His father sits in jail at this time for drug related crimes he is 37. I was telling Joshes grandfather my oldest brother and my younger sister Jane as we drove to witness the baptism. Perhaps Josh will be the one to reach his dad. This walk of Joshes is something he did all on his own with no help from his family. I also told my brother and sister on the way that I was turning into a grumpy old man. This seemed to amuse them! Yesterday morning Blue called about 6 am. I had just gotten to sleep I drank too much coffee to late the day before, I kind of felt like a tormented soul all night, wondering what my life was all about! My Dad showed up not to long after Blues phone call, so it was time for me to get up and greet the day! After Dad left I had a time of prayer. I asked God for not just for physical provision, but for supernatural provision as well. Someone stopped and got a bale of straw they left $1 in the box instead of the $5 I ask for. This made me laugh because it cost that much to get it baled! Later that day Leon the guy from New Ulm called and asked if he could come and get 3 more round bales, he paid me $140 dollars. After I left Leon I stopped by my mail box on my way to help my neighbor David plant some soybeans. I noticed a letter from my friend Steve down in Illinois. I thought I'd share in part what he wrote.

Friday
May 1st
Pekin, Illinois

Dear brother in Christ,
        I hope you're having the
Same beautiful weather we've
Been having. (I call it "world
Tomorrow-ish.")
        I'm just finishing reading
One of your 3 gift books,
you gave me last October, 2014

I'd been thinking about things
I've read. when I got out of my
car to do a job I saw this " $20"
in the gutter. Maybe it fell out
of my cluttered car. But still God,
I believe, opened my eyes to see it!
   your friend,
   Steve Geberin
Please accept this use it how so ever you may.

I knew when I read this God had answered my prayer for the day
for provision, as well as supernatural provision! Even if this was a
small thing, I believe if we cannot see God in the small things in life,
neither will we be able to see him in the greater things in life!

   Luke 16:10
   He who is faithful in what is least is faithful in what
   is much; and he who is unjust in what is least is unjust
   in what is much

In Christ,
George Denn

# EPILOG

I was plowing some ground for pumpkins the other day, my dad called to tell me he was bringing me some lunch. This struck me as odd because usually I have to phone him for such a request! He brought summer sausage sandwiches, 2 raisin cookies, and coffee. I asked him why there was only 1/4 cup of coffee? He Laughed and said he had spilled it! That statement jogged my memory and I had to laugh! At that moment I could see that my life had went full circle. Some 47 years ago a five year old boy decided to take his dad some sandwiches and coffee. Dad was cultivating corn in a field just a stone's throw from where this is written, others farm that land today. I was saddened that I had spilled the coffee on the sandwiches, but dad just laughed and, gladly ate them! I realize now that the gesture meant more than the meal! I guess that's what they mean by the circle of life! I realize I ended my 4th book with me going through a trial, but I started my 1st book with a blessing planting a new crop on a new farm. That too is the circle of life as of this year I no longer farm that place! Blessings and trials for those who follow Jesus that is the way it is! If you don't have these in your life I would question who or what you are following! After 15 years of writing stories I am not too sure there will be anymore. If there is, it's because the Holy Spirit inspired me to do so, as I feel the gift waning, but I didn't intend to write this book so when God is at work in your life anything is possible! I sure have enjoyed writing these stories' over the years, and have tried too present our triune God (God the Father, Jesus Christ, and Holy Spirit) as I see them at work in my life. For me to be the author of 4 books is nothing less than a God thing in itself! I had no intention of writing anything I am a Farmer not a writer! If you are one of the people I have meet and wrote about in the past 15 years to me it is truly an honor! Who knows where I would be today if Jesus had not been at work in my life, probably non-existent! For some reason I have become a local legend! This all came about by my following Jesus and my perception of him! I remember some girl back in grade school asking me why I always have to make such a spectacle out of myself! My friend Jeff says the pumpkin deal from start to finish is nothing less than a spectacle, so nothing much has changed! The hay, the pumpkins, the books, and anything else that I have been involved with in the past 20 years all came about by me following the legend of legends who died was buried and after three days rose from the grave and to this day is alive as can be seated at the right hand of the Father.

Hebrews 7:22- 8:2

**22** This makes Jesus the guarantee of a far better way between us and God—one that really works! A new covenant.

**23** Earlier there were a lot of priests, for they died and had to be replaced.

**24** But Jesus' priesthood is permanent. He's there from now to eternity

**25** to save everyone who comes to God through him, always on the job to speak up for them.

**26** So now we have a high priest who perfectly fits our needs: completely holy, uncompromised by sin, with authority extending as high as God's presence in heaven itself.

**27** Unlike the other high priests, he doesn't have to offer sacrifices for his own sins every day before he can get around to us and our sins. He's done it, once and for all: offered up himself as the sacrifice.

**28** The law appoints as high priests men who are never able to get the job done right. But this intervening command of God, which came later, appoints the Son, who is absolutely, eternally perfect.**1** In essence, we have just such a high priest: authoritative right alongside God,

**2** conducting worship in the one true sanctuary built by God.

I don't know how you feel but I think that dwarfs John Wayne my favorite super hero! Larger than life while alive, but still deader than a door nail! If I am viewed as anything other than a poor old farmer's son you can give Jesus the credit, and if that makes me a legend, well that's just the way it is!

I was just thinking today as I was plowing a field that so many today want to get all they can out of life. I am of the belief that others should be better off because you have lived!

The great commission.

Matthew 28:18-20

**18** Jesus, undeterred, went right ahead and gave his charge: "God authorized and commanded me to commission you:

**19**Go out and train everyone you meet, far and near, in this way of life, marking them by baptism in the threefold name: Father, Son, and Holy Spirit.

**20** Then instruct them in the practice of all I have commanded you. I'll be with you as you do this, day after day after day, right up to the end of the age."

I have found there is no better way to evangelize than to write a story. People can't argue with you if you have witnesses to the event! I encourage anyone who has a story to write it down send it forth, or a book to write to do so. You have no idea how encouraging it is to here from someone you don't even know! Write or phone you how one of your story's effected them, some even from other countries! So I hope you have enjoyed the stories as much as I have writing them. If the Holy Spirit prompts you can write too.

George Denn

59381- 243 St.

Kasota MN

56050

In closing I want to share with you a poem written by Bonnie Lindquist I received this for Christmas some years back and always wanted to us it somewhere in my stories, it looks like here is the spot.

There once was a farmer
who raised pumpkins.
He thought of himself
as just a country bumpkin.
But he was a humble man
who walked with God.
And learned lots of lessons
while working the sod.
Helping people galore
with his inspiring stories and more.
He never knows what's around the bend
or how things are going to end.
But George knows that he
can count on the Lord above.
He will survive
with his Father's Love.
God bless you all!
George W Denn

# ABOUT THE AUTHOR

G eorge W Denn now in his 53 year continues to pursue his full time farming career specializing in pumpkins that are sold on his well-known pumpkin stands around the Mankato Minnesota area! He is associated with Grace Communion International Church, and is involved with several youth camps within the denomination. He is the author of 4 books, Hey By George!, Hey By George! II on the Northwest side of Wita Lake, Hey By George! III Uncut Stones and Hey By George! IV the Legend continues.